Anthony Charles Deane

How to understand the Gospels

Anthony Charles Deane

How to understand the Gospels

ISBN/EAN: 9783337284428

Printed in Europe, USA, Canada, Australia, Japan

Cover: Foto ©Thomas Meinert / pixelio.de

More available books at **www.hansebooks.com**

HOW TO UNDERSTAND THE GOSPELS

BY

ANTHONY C. DEANE, M.A.

Vicar of All Saints, Ennismore Gardens, and
Hon. Canon of Worcester Cathedral

H&S

HODDER AND STOUGHTON
LIMITED   LONDON

Made and Printed in Great Britain.
Hazell, Watson & Viney, Ltd., London and Aylesbury.

Contents

I

THE four canonical Gospels are the greatest books in the world. Perhaps we realize this most easily if we imagine ourselves deprived of them. Suppose that these four had shared the fate of the " many " known to St. Luke, and that every copy of them had perished. Eagerly we should scrutinize the remaining New Testament books, in the vain hope of deducing from them the work, the words, the character of Jesus Christ. We should learn, indeed, that He was betrayed, instituted the eucharist on the night of betrayal, was crucified, rose from the dead, was seen of many witnesses. Beyond these bare statements we should know practically nothing. Of the Ascension alone we should possess an account, supplied by a few sentences in the Acts. That our Lord had brought a new supernatural power into the world would be evident from the amazing growth of the Church. But our guesses concerning the nature of that power, and of the way in which it became operative, must have gone hopelessly astray. Lacking the Gospels, who could have imagined such deeds and such teaching as are described in their pages ? Whether or no we count ourselves Christians, we cannot escape the influence of the Gospel ideal upon thought and conduct. And, as Christians, while we might still have without the Gospels a Lord to reverence, we should not have a Friend to love. The four little books can be given us in perhaps a hundred and fifty pages of print. They can be read from start to finish in a few hours. Yet they have shaped history to a degree almost impossible to exaggerate. As the Bible is incomparably the greatest collection of writings, so are the Gospels the supreme treasure of the Bible.

That seems obvious. Yet in the greatness of these books there are elements which we are very apt to overlook, or to take as a matter of course. Their chief glory, beyond doubt, lies in the preeminence of their theme. Whatever their form, pages which describe the life on earth of our divine Master must be unique in value and interest. When, however, this has been admitted, the marvel of the Gospels as literature ought not to be forgotten. Their writers were not conscious artists. Their simple aim, as one of them defined it in his preface, was to arrange and set down in order the facts they had received from a number of original eye-witnesses. Yet they succeeded in handling their material with a skill and sureness of touch that must amaze every literary craftsman. The episodes they describe are pictured with convincing vividness, and are never over-loaded with detail. Life-like portraits are achieved in a few words. Most wonderful, when we remember that these are Oriental writings, must seem their brevity, their reticences, their restraint. Often they have to record what transcends all normal experience, yet there is no hint of exaggeration or of fulsome comment. They state what Jesus said and did. So far as is necessary, they indicate in a phrase or two the effect of His deeds and words upon the people. And that is all. The Gospels date from an age when religious writing was almost invariably prolix and diffuse. They come from Orientals, who with any unusual experience to relate, loved to set it forth at vast length, and with wearisome insistence upon its unique character. But the Evangelists are masters of clarity and precision. They handle their material with consummate skill. They can distinguish the essential from the unimportant. They know not only what to put in but what to leave out. In Oriental writings of that date, how easily there might have been at least here and there a sentence that jarred, a fault of taste, a phrase dissonantly out of tune with the rest! From beginning to end, there is no such flaw in the Gospels. Is it superstitious to believe that the Evangelists were helped by a power more than human, were given an " inspiration of selection "? That, it must be admitted, is an old-fashioned view. Yet to readers of a trained literary sense it will seem easier and more reasonable to account for the Gospels in this way than to find any other adequate explanation of what these Evangelists were able to do.

II

Their supreme feat was their portraiture of Jesus Christ. Here, too, our familiarity with what they did must not blind us to its amazing character. The Evangelists had no patterns as their guide. There were no contemporary biographies or memoirs which they could take as models. They were creating a new kind of literature. The difficulties of their task were immense. Not the least of them must have been the embarrassing wealth of their material. If all the deeds attributed to Jesus by earlier records or spoken tradition were to be set down, " I suppose," remarked one Evangelist, " that even the world itself could not contain the books that should be written." From the mass of incidents they had to select the most important, those that typified most clearly the teaching and character of the Master. From accounts varying in detail they had to choose the most authentic. If they were to write honestly, they must record deeds and words which had astounded those who first saw and heard them, and the full meaning of which could not be clear to the Evangelists themselves. Either they must sacrifice something of candour, or they must show the Apostles at times in none too favourable a light. All such difficulties, however, were small in comparison with their chief task. By means of simple narrative they had somehow to reveal to their readers the matchless character and personality of Jesus Christ. Every other purpose of their work was subordinate to that aim, an aim so tremendous that it might have filled the greatest literary genius with despair.

And they succeeded. The influence of their Gospels on the world's history and the tribute of the simplest reader alike attest their success. Whatever else may be said of the Gospels, this is their supreme triumph. They set for ever a superb portrait of Jesus Christ before the world. It is a portrait which has compelled the homage of mankind. All the resources of literary genius could not have achieved the feat so well as did the makers of the four Gospels. The more we examine the difficulties of their task, the more remarkable will appear their success. They had so to describe the unique personality of Jesus Christ that His full and complete humanity should be evident. Yet this they had to do while making equally plain the grounds of their conviction that He was the divine Son of God. They had to leave the reader sure that He was both sorely tempted and morally perfect. They had to give an impression of His charm and of His strength, of His power of withering invective, of the tenderness which drew the little children to Him, of His unerring insight into character, of His matchless sympathy. They had to show Him scorned, solitary, homeless, yet quietly asserting claims that, coming from any teacher merely human, would have been insufferably arrogant.

If one Evangelist had contrived in his few chapters to draw a convincing picture of our Lord, the fact would have been notable. But that all four should have succeeded, and that their four pictures should be in essential agreement, is far more wonderful. No doubt Matthew and Luke borrowed from Mark, or from earlier documents incorporated in Mark. No doubt, too, the style of the Fourth Gospel, its balance of emphasis, and the character of the teaching it attributes to Jesus, are sharply different from those of the earlier three. The Fourth Gospel surveys the work of the Master from another point of view. Again, there are evident differences

between the three synoptists. The special
aim and personal bias of the Matthew
editor and Luke cause them to arrange and
modify with some freedom the material
they have taken over from Mark. More
striking, in consequence, is the truth that
the portrait of Jesus Christ Himself is
essentially the same in all four Gospels.
Where one supplies what is lacking in the
others, it is a detail perfectly congruous
with those already known. We are never
made to feel, for instance, that the Jesus
of Luke is other than the Jesus of Mark.
The teaching chronicled by John is different,
but the Teacher is the same. That each of
the Evangelists gives us clearly a convincing portrait, and that the portrait of
all is essentially one, must seem a fact the
more impressive the more we ponder it.
If, primarily, the Gospels are great because
of their unique theme, they are great also
because they are without parallel as
literature.

That greatness becomes more apparent
when we contrast the four with the numerous
" apocryphal gospels " written from the
middle of the second century onwards.
Some of these combined authentic history

from the canonical Gospels with legends. Some were fabricated to support a special theory. Thus there were people anxious to believe that our Lord could suffer no real pain, and the so-called " Gospel of Peter " was written to give colour to this view. The largest fragment of it we possess was dug up in Egypt in 1886. It contains a description of the Crucifixion and Resurrection. Jesus, we are told, did not die, but was miraculously " taken up " from the Cross. In manuscripts now at Hereford and the British Museum is an account of the Birth of Christ which also may come, as the Provost of Eton has recently argued with great cogency,[1] from this " Gospel of Peter." At the time of the Birth a bright light is seen which gradually takes the form of an infant. The child has no weight, and His eyes dazzle those who look at them. A number of other apocryphal gospels record fantastic stories of the birth and boyhood of Jesus. He makes twelve sparrows of clay, which come to life and fly when He claps His hands.[2] A boy who runs up

[1] *Latin Infancy Gospels*, edited by M. R. James (Camb. University Press, 1927).

[2] *Gospel of Thomas.*

against Him falls dead.[1]   A youth has been changed by witchcraft into a mule ; when Mary places Jesus on the mule's back it disappears, and the young man stands in its place.[2]   When Mary with her child enters an Egyptian temple, the idols bow down.[3]   These are but a few from a vast number of such stories.   Their atmosphere is like that of *The Arabian Nights.*   Worthless as they are in themselves, they help us to realize the kind of thing which appealed to the readers of that age.   And the difference between them and the four canonical Gospels is exceedingly impressive.   It heightens our immense gratitude to the Evangelists, who did not merely put together Gospels, but kept them free from every trace of fantasy.   As we examine their sober pages, we feel that their witness is true.   The ultimate message of our religion comes to us in a perfect setting, and the Gospels, wonderful in what they relate, are wonderful also in their manner of relating it.   They are indeed the greatest books in the world.

[1] *Gospel of Thomas.*
[2] *Arabic Gospel of the Childhood.*
[3] *Gospel of Pseudo-Matthew.*

III

Here, then, they are, preserved for us through eighteen centuries. As a help to understanding them, we need to ask the same questions as would occur to us before reading any other documents of extreme antiquity. At what time, and in what circumstances, came they to be written? What do we know for certain of their authorship and their authors? For what readers were they first designed? How is it that they are four, that one was not thought sufficient, or that one of them did not supersede the other three? In what relation of time and trustworthiness do they stand to one another? Are the divergences between them fundamental, and do they invalidate their trustworthiness? Is each the work of a single author or a compilation? Are the Gospels as we possess them the Gospels as they were originally written, or as they were subsequently edited? Successive generations of scholars have toiled patiently to answer such questions. If some points are still, and seem likely to remain, in dispute, there are many in regard to which definite con-

2

clusions have been reached. And their importance is hardly realized as yet by the general Bible-reading public. If the study of them is necessarily technical, the results arrived at have much more than a merely literary or antiquarian interest. We are helping ourselves to read the Gospels intelligently, and the precise force of their spiritual message will be plainer, if we put ourselves so far as possible in the position of their first readers. By doing that we shall avoid misinterpretations that are far too common. Indeed, any study which adds to the interest and perception with which we examine these unique writings must be evidently worth while.

We begin, then, by trying to realize the conditions in which the earliest Gospels took shape. Probably that was not until many years after the Ascension. During the life on earth of our Lord some of His disciples may have noted for themselves accounts of His words and deeds, and such notes may have been utilized later when a " Gospel," as we now use that term, was to be written. That is, however, no more than a possibility ; we are quite without evidence about it. What seems certain is

that all the letters of St. Paul are earlier
in date than any of our four Gospels. In
the first years of Christianity there would be
no need for a detailed account in writing
of our Lord's ministry. For one thing,
vivid memories could be obtained in talk
with those who had been eye-witnesses of
His work. When Christians came together,
one or another would relate what he himself
had seen Jesus do, would pass on the
teaching he himself had heard. And, for
another thing, it seemed superfluous at
that time to put together a written Gospel
in order that it might be handed on to later
generations. The Christians of that age
believed there would be no later generations.
" This generation shall not pass till all
these things be fulfilled " they misinterpreted as a promise of the Lord's return
within their lifetime. Even when, about
twenty-two years after the Ascension,
1 Thessalonians—in all probability the
earliest of the New Testament books—
was written, that belief coloured deeply
the thought of the Church.

But year followed year, and it became
evident that the end was not to be yet.
The number still surviving of those who

had been eye-witnesses of Christ's ministry rapidly diminished. Soon none would be left. Clearly it was desirable that their first-hand testimony should be collated and set down in writing. Otherwise some of the true tradition might be forgotten, while unauthentic stories or inaccurate recollections of what others had told might be mingled with it. Again, so long as the return of Jesus Christ, and with it the end of this world, were supposed to be imminent, the affairs of this life, its relationships and problems of conduct, seemed of little importance. But they became acutely pressing again when it grew certain that one Christian generation after another must still play its part on earth. Hitherto Christian doctrine, as we see from the Acts and St. Paul's letters, had almost limited itself to setting forth the death, Resurrection, and return of our Lord. Now, however, came a natural wish to know more of His teaching. Here were the problems of earthly life ; how had He viewed them ? What counsel had He given ? How had He Himself lived and done before the Crucifixion ? A written Gospel, a story of His life, and a summary of His practical instructions about conduct, became an obvious need. And accordingly it was a need which at this stage, St. Luke tells us, many writers attempted to supply.

IV

· By this time, too—roughly about thirty years after the Ascension—the Christian Church had not only increased vastly in numbers but undergone an essential change in character. There are still people who imagine vaguely that the Church came into being, or at least was given definite shape, in consequence of what was written in the Gospels. So it may be not quite superfluous to remind ourselves that this is to reverse the true order. The Church had been in existence for a whole generation before the earliest of our Gospels was written. It was the Church which brought the Gospels into existence, not the Gospels which brought the Church. And recent changes and developments within the Church accentuated the need which the Gospels were written to satisfy.

For Christianity in its first days (and this fact, too, seems seldom understood by the general reader) was a form of Judaism.

The first Christians were Jews by religion as well as by race. They did not renounce Judaism when they accepted Jesus as the Messiah. All that they did was to identify the Messiah, in the promise of whose coming every Jew believed, with Him. Those Jews who thus thought of Jesus of Nazareth formed a kind of guild within the Jewish Church. They used baptism as the sign of admission into this guild. They held their guild meetings in private houses for prayer and the eucharist—the solemn " breaking of the bread." But as yet they had no thought of any severance from their national religion. As a matter of course they had their sons circumcised, they took part in the Temple services, they upheld strict obedience to the Law as the chief essential of righteousness. As yet they could not imagine that God would have direct relationship except with His chosen people. Yet their belief in Jesus as the Christ made the fraternal spirit among this Jerusalem guild very strong. It led them to make an experiment of communal ownership. Before long that experiment proved a disastrous failure, but its beginning was bright enough. The last sentences of Acts

ii. picture the life of the guild: "Day by day, continuing stedfastly with one accord in the temple, and breaking bread at home, they did take their food with gladness and singleness of heart, praising God, and having favour with all the people. And the Lord added to them day by day those that were being saved."

"Having favour with all the people" needs qualification. The Sadducees were hostile, because this new sect made much of the doctrine of resurrection, a doctrine which the Sadducees bitterly opposed, as having no place in the original Law. The opening of Acts iv. records how "the Sadducees came upon" Peter and John, "being sore troubled because they taught the people and proclaimed in Jesus the resurrection from the dead." But the small and aristocratic sect of the Sudducees was doubtless not included among "the people" of St. Luke's sentence. The general body of Jews did believe in a resurrection, and they had no quarrel with their fellow-Jews who had joined the Christian guild. So long as these duly upheld the Law and the traditions, the addition to their creed seemed of little importance. To accept

Jesus as the promised Messiah was a strange error, yet, in itself, a harmless error.

This attitude, however, did not long persist. It was changed abruptly by the teaching of Stephen, which implied that the new faith must supersede the Law, and that the Law itself had served only as a step towards fuller revelation. This was an affront not to the Sadducees only, but to the Pharisees, and indeed to the whole creed of Judaism, which accounted the Law as the final revelation. Stephen was promptly condemned to death. All who accepted Jesus as Messiah, since they did not dissociate themselves from Stephen's views, were persecuted. In consequence, they fled from Jerusalem and were scattered throughout Judea and Samaria. Afterwards they went farther afield. And, as a result, Christianity made new converts in new regions.

Yet the old conflict of ideals was not ended. To understand its severity is to get the key to the Acts and many of St. Paul's letters. We shall observe, for instance, with what difficulty St. Peter came over to the new view that Christianity was to be a world-religion, and a religion independent of Judaism. We shall see how immense was the task of St. Paul in persuading his converts that Gentiles need not be circumcised as Jewish proselytes in order to belong to the Church. Gradually the view for which he stood prevailed. Christianity became an independent religion, not a mere cult within Judaism. The work begun by the disciples of Stephen was developed by St. Paul and his companions. From Jerusalem the doctrine was carried through Palestine, from Palestine through Asia Minor, from Asia Minor to Greece and Rome. Its headquarters, from which missions were sent out, soon became Antioch in Syria, instead of Jerusalem. And the new wide appeal of Christianity was typified by the fact that such a city as Antioch became, in a sense, its centre. Here Jewish, Greek, and Oriental elements mingled. It was a city, to borrow Dr. A. E. J. Rawlinson's description,[1] " in whose streets and colonnades and bazaars a bewildering variety of human types— Greek, Syrian, Anatolian, Chaldæan, Arabian, Jew—met and jostled and talked and gesticulated and bargained and exchanged

[1] In his Bampton Lectures, 1926.

ideas in the vulgar colloquial Greek which, as a result of the conquests of Alexander and by the policy of his successors, had become the common medium of intercourse in the Levant." This picture helps us to understand why the colloquial Greek of that age—the *koiné*, as it was called—was, instead of Aramaic, the language in which our Gospels were written. Aramaic was still the spoken language of the Palestinian Jews. But they knew Greek also, and Greek was understood, as Aramaic was not, by the mass of people elsewhere. Indeed, it seemed a providential thing that, at the time when the Gospels were to be written, a language familiar to men of a vast number of races, an almost international language, should have been available for the writers.

V

In such conditions, then, the first three of our Gospels were put together for the Church. Perhaps that phrase should be recast if it is not to mislead ; they were made for local branches of the Church. These were not abstract compositions thrown, so to speak, into the air ; each was undertaken to suit the needs of one particular set of people—or, in the instance of the third Gospel, possibly even for the needs of one particular person—at a special time. We must use our imaginations to realize the circumstances of that age, when travel was slow and hazardous, when it was impossible to multiply rapidly copies of a document, when a Gospel must laboriously be written, letter by letter, on a roll of papyrus some thirty feet long.

The organization of the Church was as yet of the simplest kind. Each local branch was virtually a self-contained unit. In towns which St. Paul or another missioner had visited—Antioch, Ephesus, Philippi, Corinth, Rome, and very many more—a branch of the Church had been formed. In course of time a certain number of migrants from other places would be added to it. Any Christian who came to live in the place, or, as a trader, was there temporarily on business, would attach himself to the local church. Sometimes he would bring a gift or a message from another church. He would describe its ways and its services, and thus there would be an interchange of ideas. The members would meet regularly on the first day of the week.

As there were as yet no Christian Church buildings, they would gather in any large house available for the purpose. To watch the men and women who entered must have convinced the most casual onlooker that this new religion had a unifying power without parallel. Among the Christian community were people of many races, who in their earlier days had belonged to many different religions. Jew and Gentile came together, members of various professions and callings, rich and poor, learned and illiterate, the slave-owner and the slave.

At their meeting on the first day of the week the eucharist would be celebrated, followed often by a common meal. Set prayers would be used, and often extracts from the Old Testament. Churches which had received a letter from St. Paul would cause a portion of it to be read aloud for practical instruction ; as yet there was no idea, of course, of ranking the epistles as " scripture." But they were written in order that their messages might be made public at gatherings of the church addressed. Thus the co-called " Epistle to the Ephesians " was really a circular letter sent to the church in each of the chief towns in Asia ; it got its name later because the copy of this circular letter that was sent to Ephesus happened to be the copy that survived.

And at meetings of the local churches everywhere there would be a keen eagerness, we may be sure, to learn all that could be told of what Jesus Christ had done and taught. Those who had received in past years any trustworthy tradition from eye-witnesses would declare it. But stronger and stronger became the feeling that, both for themselves, and still more for the sake of those to come after, some definite book of the Gospel of Jesus Christ, based upon the best evidence, and collated with any fragmentary records already in existence, should be provided for the use of the local church. Local circumstances would naturally affect its shape. Thus a branch of the Church with many Jewish members would welcome details to illustrate how the deeds of Jesus corresponded with those which prophecy had assigned to the Messiah. But such points would have little interest for another branch of the Church elsewhere, whose members were Gentiles.

So the Gospels came to be written.

I

EVEN if he knew nothing of technical scholarship or Biblical " criticism," every careful reader of the Gospels would be impressed by two facts : one, that the Fourth Gospel is very different from the first three ; the other, that the first three are very alike. Differences, plainly, there are. Each gives us some incidents not recorded by either of the other two, and each has its own characteristics of style and treatment. That is what we should expect in three books by three authors. What we should not expect is to find in three separate Gospels long passages identical in their wording, or so nearly identical that the resemblance cannot be due to chance. It would have seemed likely enough that actual sayings of Christ should have been treasured in the memory of those who heard them, and passed on with careful precision to those who came after. It would have seemed reasonable that main facts of crucial importance should have been told and retold in virtually the same words. Verbal memory was far stronger in ages before the invention of printing had rendered it less essential, and the training of the verbal memory formed a chief part of Hebrew education. Inability to understand a saying was no bar to remembering what had been said. Indeed, as a modern commentator [1] has observed, it had the opposite effect. The Apostles and first teachers were "sometimes stronger in memory than in understanding. They remembered what perplexed them, *because* it perplexed them; and they reported it faithfully."

That there was in the earliest days a spoken tradition of what our Lord had done and said seems certain. By this fact scholars of a past generation accounted for the verbal identities in the first three Gospels. Each Evangelist, they supposed, had reproduced the spoken tradition in writing. But further study showed this explanation to be inadequate. It is not only in describing the main facts, or in reporting the words of Christ, that these

[1] Dr. Plummer, in his *St. Matthew*, p. 10.

identities occur. They extend frequently to small details in the narrative, which could hardly have been crystallized into one precise form of words. These identities, or close resemblances, when describing details, are so numerous that we must believe the earliest of the three Gospels to have been utilized by the authors of the other two, or that all three had some written sources in common before them as they worked. A modern analogy, suggested by Dr. Streeter, may be used to illustrate the point. We look, let us suppose, at an account of the same football match in three different newspapers. The main facts —i.e. the result, the number of goals, the names of the men who scored them— will be the same in all accounts. Yet the detailed description of the play, if it be written by three independent reporters, will be worded quite differently in the three newspapers. If, on the contrary, we find the match described in almost identical language, with only slight omissions and variations, by each newspaper, we know that each has obtained its material from the common source—a report supplied by a news-agency—and that the varia-

tions are due to the newspaper sub-
editors.

That is a crude and prosaic illustration,
yet it serves to describe the impression left
with the student who examines carefully
our first three Gospels. In each is something of the Evangelist's own, each supplies
something found in none of the others.
Sometimes, as in the Gospel of Mark, it
may have been derived from the writer's
personal experience. Sometimes it may
have been obtained from a record, spoken
or written, to which none of the other
Evangelists had access. Apart, however,
from this original element in each Gospel,
there is also in each a large proportion which
has been taken from sources common to
them all. Sometimes the author seems to
have transcribed an earlier document without change ; more often, while following
it in the main, he has abridged it here and
there, or altered its wording or interpolated
an explanation.

What, then, are the relations between
the first three Gospels ? The Fourth clearly
stands apart, both in time and character.
We will postpone the questions which arise
concerning it until we come to the chapters

3

dealing specially with this Gospel of John.
But the other three are connected, and have
much the same standpoint. A name im-
plying this common point of view has been
given them, and they are termed the
" synoptic " Gospels. In what degree are
they interdependent? Which is the earliest?
From which have the others in part been
copied? What other common sources of
information can we detect in them? How
are we to account for the identities and the
differences in their narratives?

II

Questions of this kind constitute what is
known as the " synoptic problem." Immense pains have been spent upon it, and
the literature on the subject, mostly technical
in character, is voluminous. The general
reader may feel that such researches,
fascinating as they may seem to experts,
do not much interest him, and that he need
not trouble about them in order to understand and profit by the Gospels. Up to a
point, of course, that is quite true. He
cannot fairly be asked to concern himself
with the minute processes of technical

scholarship. On the other hand, he will find it well worth while to know something of the results. Not only have they a good deal of human interest, but they supply a real help to reading the Gospels intelligently.

A good many people, too, are haunted by a rather vague idea that " modern criticism " has in some way weakened the authority of the Gospels and made them less credible. Nothing can allay that fear so effectively as to know what the results of criticism really are. No other writings in the world have been scrutinized so minutely. Every sentence, almost every word, in them has been considered from every point of view. The tests of literature, archæology, and comparative religion have been applied to them. They have been approached, from one extreme, by champions of an impossible theory of literal inspiration, and, from the other, by opponents eager to discredit beliefs they are already determined to reject. From such ordeals the Gospels have emerged triumphantly. No one can pretend that all the " critical problems " have been solved, or indeed are capable of solution. We may feel that some of the theories advanced concerning them are far more convincing and satisfactory than others, yet theories, not proven facts, all must remain. Again, there are seeming discrepancies in the different Gospels for which, with our limited knowledge, we cannot account. There are occasional phrases the precise force of which is still uncertain. Yet modern research, and particularly the vastly improved acquaintance with Greek of the New Testament period, brought by the discovery and study of papyri, has definitely cleared up many points which, even half a century ago, seemed hopelessly obscure. And the main fact is that all this critical work, all this added knowledge, all this minute investigation of the Gospels, have strengthened, not diminished, their general trustworthiness as historical documents. "Modern criticism" has made it more, not less, reasonable to believe in that Person and work of Jesus Christ which the Gospels were written to set forth.

From these general considerations let us turn back to the "synoptic problem." As I have said, the general reader cannot be expected to trouble himself with the details of the immense literature that has been written about it or with the processes by which scholars have reached their conclusions. Yet to know the results themselves is well worth his while. As he observes the likenesses and differences in the first three Gospels, the reader will naturally want to know how these are explained by the best authorities. If that information can be given him in a short and simple form, certainly it should help him to understand the Gospels.

III

The " oral-tradition " theory—the theory that, before they were written, the Gospel stories were told in a fixed form of words, that much of this form was incorporated afterwards in the written Gospels, and that their frequent identity of wording is thus explained—has already been mentioned, with some of the reasons for which it was found unconvincing. It was superseded by what was known as the " two-document " theory, and this held the field until quite recently.

Briefly summarized, the " two-document " theory about the synoptic Gospels was as follows. Mark [1] is the earliest of the Gospels. The authors of Matthew and Luke had Mark before them when they wrote, and made extensive use of it. In fact, of the 660 verses in Mark, no fewer than 610, it is said, have been used by Matthew, or Luke, or both. But then students observed that there is also much material in both Matthew and Luke which is absent from Mark. In the main, this material is composed of "sayings" of Christ, whereas Mark is more concerned to record His deeds than His words. The accounts of these discourses in Matthew and Luke are so much alike that they seem to have been derived from the same document. Therefore the critics took it as proved that such a document, a collection of our Lord's words, must have existed, though no copy of it survives. This document they named "Q." Further, there was, of course, in both Matthew and Luke some original matter, some information peculiar to the one Evangelist. In broad outline, then,

[1] For the sake of clearness, throughout I prefix "St." to the name of an Evangelist when the reference is to the man, but not when it is to his book. Thus "St. Luke" means the Evangelist, "Luke" the Gospel he wrote.

and omitting subsidiary developments, the theory held that when Matthew and Luke were to be written, the material that each Evangelist had was : (*a*) special information of his own, and (*b*) two documents—St. Mark's Gospel, and " Q." Such was the " two-document " synoptic theory.

It was accepted, either in this form or with minor variations, by the great majority of scholars in England and America until 1924.[1] In that year a new theory was propounded by Dr. B. H. Streeter, of Oxford. He himself had previously held the " two-document " theory. But, as the result of immense study, he had ulti-mately found himself obliged to replace it by a " four-document " theory. He still believed that Mark and " Q " had been used by Matthew and Luke. Close examination of these two later Gospels, however, had enabled him to identify in them the use of two other documents. In Matthew he detected the use of an early Judaistic account of Christ's teaching, which he names " M." St. Luke, Dr.

---

[1] Under their influence, I adopted the " two-docu-ment " theory when writing, in 1923, the chapter on The Synoptic Gospels in *How to Enjoy the Bible*.

Streeter believes, rewrote the present Gospel from an earlier form of it, which in turn he had amplified from a first sketch. That first sketch he calls " L." According to the " four-document " hypothesis, therefore, Matthew used Mark, " Q," and " M " ; Luke used Mark, " Q," and " L." No such bald statement, however, can give any just idea of the laborious analysis which Dr. Streeter has made, of the subtleties of his reconstructions, or the wealth of detail by which he seeks to uphold them. Of permanent value, wholly apart from his theories, is his emphasis of the truth that each Gospel was originally local in character, adapted for the use of a local branch of the Church.

Dr. Streeter's " four-document " hypothesis has gained a large measure of acceptance among English-speaking scholars. In Germany, since the war, attempts have been made to analyse the contents of the Gospel by a new method—or, to speak more precisely, by a method only employed hitherto in the study of folk-lore. This method returns, in some degree, to the " oral-tradition " theory. It holds that there were current in the first days of the Church traditions of our Lord's teaching grouped according to subject and form ; one group of His apocalyptic sayings, another of His practical exhortations, and so forth, and that these groups of sayings, originally collected for oral teaching, are the main material of the written Gospels. The critics of this school seem as yet to be considerably at variance among themselves, and their views have not gained many adherents outside Germany. It is rather strange, however, that Dr. Streeter ignores them entirely.

The weakness of the *formgeschichtliche* method of criticism is the rather impossibly rigid rules of form which it endeavours to lay down. That weakness is avoided by the " multiple-document " theory.[1] Both the " two-document " theory and the " four-document " hypothesis developed from it are open to far weightier objections than Dr. Streeter allows his readers to suppose. Both are based upon the supposition that Matthew and Luke used " Q " and Mark. But the very existence of

[1] One of its principal exponents, Professor Torm, of Copenhagen, gave an admirable summary of it in the *Church Quarterly*, July 1927.

"Q," we must remember, is purely a hypothesis. As Dr. Torm remarks, "the more the critics insist on ' Q ' as a large independent source, the more surprising is it that it is altogether lost." And, to take a far weightier point, while we emphasize the apparent quotations from Mark in Matthew and Luke, what are we to make of the omissions ? Of a long connected group of narratives, found in Mark vi. 45–viii. 26, nothing is found in Luke. Dr. Streeter's attempt to explain this is that Luke had a " mutilated copy of Mark " before him. Other ingenious yet unconvincing attempts have been made to account for the omission of other shorter passages. The real difficulty, however, which neither the " two-document " critics nor Dr. Streeter frankly recognize, lies in the fact that there are a very large number of details, often vivid and life-like details, given by Mark, and omitted by *both* Matthew and Luke. Had they been left out by one or other of these Evangelists, writing with Mark before him, we might have wondered at the reason. But we have far more cause to be surprised when, supposing them both to be copying from Mark, both Matthew and Luke omit the same details. That by mere chance they should have left out precisely the same things—Professor Torm gives more than twenty examples—does, indeed, seem incredible.

One attempted explanation is that " Mark " as we have it is not the original Gospel of Mark, the document which Matthew and Luke copied, but a later and enlarged edition. That explanation breaks down, because the details omitted by Matthew and Luke are eminently characteristic of Mark, and cannot be later interpolations.

IV

From all this tangle of intricate and subtle conjectures, is there any escape to a simpler explanation which will meet the facts ? The answer seems to be that there is, if we can be bold enough to get clear away from that " two-document " theory which for so long held the field, and also from the " four-document " theory into which Dr. Streeter's ingenuity has amplified it. Then, not without a sense of relief, we can get rid of " Q," that mysteriously vanished document. The theories of the critics brought it into hypothetical being ; if we can replace those theories, we can escape the need of imagining " Q."

As it happens, one of the synoptists does describe the "sources" from which his own Gospel was compiled. We have that account in the first four verses of Luke. St. Luke states that already "many" people have set their hands to writing down the established facts of the Christian record. He and the others have received traditions (spoken or written) from those who had been actual eye-witnesses of our Lord's ministry. Therefore, having carefully examined and collated all these earlier narratives and traditions, he has resolved to arrange them methodically in a Gospel of his own. Here, accordingly, are St. Luke's materials : (*a*) written Gospels, whole or fragmentary ; (*b*) through them, and probably apart from them as well, the evidence of eye-witnesses ; to which we doubtless must add (*c*) information which St. Luke had collected independently for himself.

This account of his materials and his use of them comes, let us remember, from St. Luke. It is not a modern theory. We may well believe that the method of one of the synoptists was, more or less, the method of the other two, and that they also were acquainted with some of the " many " written narratives mentioned by St. Luke. Individual versions would vary, each would have some which the other two had not ; each would make his own choice of material, and when the document used happened to be in Aramaic, two or three Evangelists would not use precisely the same Greek words when translating it. We are no longer driven to suppose that Matthew and Luke borrowed directly from Mark—a theory which, as we have seen, involves great difficulties. A close similarity, or identity, in two Gospels means that in this passage both writers were utilizing the same earlier document. Again, to quote Professor Torm, " we reach the most natural explanation of the fact that Mark vi. 45–viii. 26 is not found in Luke by supposing that this passage, originally constituting a small independent group of accounts, dropped into the hands of two of the Evangelists, but not of Luke." Instead, rhen, of believing, as do the supporters both of the " two-document " and " four-document " hypothesis, that the chief

sources of Matthew and Luke are Mark
and a conjectured document called " Q,"
those preferring the " multiple-document "
hypothesis believe that Mark, Matthew, and
Luke alike were based on some of those
" many " earlier Gospels, or fragments of
Gospels, to which St. Luke refers in his
preface.

Time only can show whether the " multiple-document " theory (linked, possibly,
with the less extravagant of the " form "
theories now popular among German
scholars) will be accepted as the best
solution of the " synoptic problem." But
it would be disingenuous to conceal from
the reader that at present it is the " four-
document " hypothesis, supported as it is
by the brilliant scholarship of Dr. Streeter,
which secures the adherence of most English-
speaking scholars.

V

Though it is only in the barest outlines
that I have tried to sketch the " synoptic
problem " and the chief of its attempted
solutions, some of my readers may feel
that, so far as they are concerned, the whole
business is tedious and unprofitable.

" Surely it is unnecessary," they will say,
" that we should concern ourselves with the
technical controversies of academic experts.
Surely we need not pay attention to such
matters in order to understand the Gospels,
in order to appreciate rightly their spiritual
teaching or their literary charm. Again,
if we are to believe that the Evangelists
were inspired, is not all this talk about
' sources ' beside the point ? " One can
understand such remonstrances, and, in a
degree, sympathize with them. Yet I
still dare to hope that, in retrospect, the
reader will admit this rather dull chapter
to have been well worth while. For to
know something of the kind of way in which
the Gospels were put together clears away
at once a whole host of difficulties which
otherwise we should encounter, one by
one, as we read their narratives. Remembering the composite nature of the Gospels,
we shall not be perplexed by what seem
like small errors or inconsistencies. The
real marvel is that they should be so few.
Again, all educated people have heard of
the " synoptic problem," yet often speak
of criticism in almost total ignorance of
its real results. It will be a gain, if, without

going into linguistic and other details, they can have some idea of the principal lines modern criticism has taken and the principal theories it holds. As to inspiration, we may ponder again St. Luke's Preface. It shows that an inspired writer thought care and research essential in order to secure accuracy.

But from all such preliminary thoughts and studies we will turn now to the Gospels themselves. In the Bible, Matthew stands first ; possibly because its frequent references to the Prophets seemed to make it a link between the Old Testament and the New. There is, however, practical unanimity among scholars in believing Mark to be the earliest of our Gospels. With Mark, accordingly, we will begin. I hope that the reader will keep an open copy of the Bible—or, at least, of the New Testament— beside him ; all that my book can try to do is to help him to read the Gospels for himself with fuller understanding.

So, in all reverence, we turn to these, the greatest writings in the world.

I

In the first century the meeting of the local Church in Rome must have been extraordinarily varied and picturesque. On the further side of the Tiber there had long been a Jewish colony. It began when Pompey brought a batch of prisoners from Jerusalem in 69 B.C. They showed the characteristics of their race. Within four or five years they had become a free community, to whose growing numbers and great influence Cicero referred. Jews from Rome were in Jerusalem on the day of Pentecost. They may have become converts to Christianity and have spread the new faith on their return. Certainly when, about twenty-five years later, St. Paul wrote his letter to the Church in Rome, it had been in existence for a considerable time and had, as his language shows, a wide repute. He is careful to express his reluctance even to

4   49

seem to "build upon another man's foundation"; a phrase according well with the ancient tradition that the real pioneer of the Church in Rome was St. Peter. His name, and the Lord's phrase about basing the Church on that rock, give an obvious aptness to St. Paul's sentence. St. Paul's imprisonment in Rome proved to be, as he said, "for the furtherance of the Gospel" there, and he brought into its brotherhood persons so dissimilar as a fugitive slave and members of the Prætorian Guard. But there is no ground for doubting the widespread and well-supported belief that St. Peter spent his last years continuously in Rome, and presided over the Christian church in that city.

How strange a spectacle that society must have presented when it met each first day of the week! Here Roman citizens of aristocratic families mingled with slaves; here Gentiles knelt beside Jews. Nowhere was the unifying power of this new creed, in which "bond and free, circumcision and uncircumcision," were merged, shown more effectively and pictorially than in the capital of the Roman Empire. So they met, and, sacrament and prayers ended, gathered, with an eagerness we can well imagine, round St. Peter. When he spoke, they were listening to one who had been in close companionship with the Lord, one who could tell what he himself had heard and seen, to whom the Master had appeared after the Resurrection. How anxious their questions, how close their attention ! And how often they must have said among themselves : " Ought not one of us to put down in writing these marvellous reminiscences ? Then we could get them into due sequence, and study them at leisure, and use them when we are trying to make new converts, and hand them on to those who shall follow us."

Many may have made that suggestion. It was John Mark who carried it out. The affectionate intimacy between him and the aged Apostle is shown in the First Epistle of Peter, where the younger man is described as " Mark, my son." Papias, who wrote what he had been told by a contemporary of St. Mark, and himself is quoted by Eusebius, the first Church historian, states that " Mark, having become Peter's interpreter," set down all that the Apostle remembered of what Christ had said or done. But these memories were not then in chronological order. They were written down as spoken, except that it was the work of the " interpreter " to write them in Greek. Mark could not originate them, " for he," Papias adds, " neither heard the Lord nor followed Him ; but later was with Peter, who suited his teaching to his hearer's needs, not as describing our Lord's sayings in strict sequence." Papias—or, rather, the earlier authority he quotes—goes on to emphasize the extreme care and accuracy with which St. Mark wrote down what he had heard. This, among the earliest of Christian traditions, is confirmed by other second-century writers.

One of them, Irenæus, says it was after Peter's death that " Mark, the disciple and interpreter of Peter, handed down to us in writing the things that Peter preached." But we need not trouble ourselves, as some commentators have done, over the supposed discrepancy between what Papias says was done in St. Peter's lifetime and what Irenæus says was done after his death. The two sentences describe different stages. Look again at Papias's account. How true to life it is ! St. Peter did not deliver by instalments a systematic Gospel. He drew from his store of memories what his hearers wanted. " Let us hear again about the Crucifixion," they would say on one day ; perhaps on the next : " Let us hear how you were first called to discipleship." So St. Peter gave them, not a serial narrative continued from day to day, but, as an old man will, detached memories as they came back to him, or as his hearers' questions or comments prompted. And close beside him, noting it all, was John Mark, who thus gradually compiled a manuscript he might have headed " Stray Recollections of an Apostle." That was the first stage.

The second came after St. Peter's death. Then John Mark resolved to put together a Gospel. There were many reasons why he should wish now to do this. A new generation was growing up. Few were left of those who actually had witnessed the Master's work on earth. Evangelists who preached Christianity needed an authentic record of its historic facts. Congregations which met for worship could hear St. Peter no more, but what he had spoken could be arranged in order and read to them. As

a pretence for the persecution which Nero
had set afoot in Rome, many gross false-
hoods were circulated concerning the
Founder of Christianity. They could be
refuted best by a trustworthy narrative
of His ministry. And there were some
Christians who mistakenly thought they
could emphasize His divinity by denying
His full humanity. The Gospel shows
St. Mark's evident anxiety to prove the
real manhood of the divine Master.

II

What were the materials out of which
the Evangelist could make his book ?
First, there was the record he had made
of St. Peter's reminiscences. Then there
were other short documents, which, or other
versions of which, were utilized later by the
writers of Matthew and Luke. And, by
no means least, he had personal recollections
of his own upon which to draw, for, as
we shall see, there is good reason to think
that he had been in Jerusalem through the
week of our Lord's Passion, and had been
an eye-witness of its events. Yet for this
time also he would have obtained much

information from St. Peter, whose spoken reminiscences of it must have contained many details which only one of the Twelve could supply.

The work of comparing, revising, and arranging all this material cannot have been light, and to decide what should be omitted must have needed anxious consideration. The "dates" of the Gospels cannot be given with precision ; there has been, and probably always will be, differing opinions among scholars concerning them. If, however, St. Mark did not write his book until after St. Peter's death, as Irenæus states, in all probability it was not written before the year 64. For that is the year when Nero began the persecution of the Christians in Rome which brought about, as tradition affirms, St. Peter's martyrdom. On the other hand, the Gospel seems earlier than the fall of Jerusalem in the year 70. Yet a note in chapter xiii, verse 14, looks as if it were written when the fall of the city was imminent, though we cannot be sure that this note was not interpolated by some copyist. "Somewhere between 64 and 70 A.D." is perhaps as near as we can go in trying to fix the "date" of St. Mark, and even then we are short of anything like certainty.

But discussions about the " date " of a Gospel are often misleading to the general reader. Even skilled critics seem apt to forget how limited a meaning the word can have. In modern conditions, the year printed on the title-page of a new book may be considerably distant from the time when the contents were first put down on paper. It does show, however, when the book was published, and thereby made available for any readers who chose to buy it. There was no counterpart to that stage in the history of the Gospels. They were not published. They were designed in the first instance for the use of a small group of people in one place. St. Luke, indeed, seems to have written his for a single reader, Theophilus. Thus the " date " of a Gospel cannot mean the time when it came before the world, but only the time when the writing out of the original, letter by letter, on a roll of papyrus was finished. Indefinitely later the document might be used for reading aloud at meetings of the local church. Afterwards a day might come when some traveller who wished to make this Gospel known to his own local church would employ a scribe to copy it. That is the only sort of " publication " a Gospel could have ; that is the kind of way in which first it became known outside the place of its origin. If the original roll of papyrus (a very fragile thing) were mutilated before any transcription had been made, then all the copies of it would be imperfect.

The last point has a special significance in the instance of St. Mark's book. Either he left it unfinished through death, illness, or imprisonment, or else part of the roll on which he set down his Gospel was torn away before any copy of it had been made. For, as it has come down to us, Mark breaks off abruptly, with an unfinished sentence, at the eighth verse of the final chapter.[1] The twelve verses in our English Bible that follow are no true part of St. Mark's work. As a marginal note in the Revised Version states, they are not found in the oldest manuscripts of the Gospel that have

[1] Of course, the division into " chapters " and " verses " was made long afterwards, for the sake of convenience in reference ; there were no such divisions in the early MSS.

survived.[1] They represent one of a number of endings written by unknown hands in early days in order to fill the gap and round off the story left unfinished by St. Mark. Dr. Streeter suggests that, as this was pre-eminently the " Gospel of Peter," stories of Resurrection appearances to St. Peter would naturally find a place in it, and that chapter xxi of the Fourth Gospel, evidently added as a supplement to that work, was based upon the "lost" ending of Mark. But this is, of course, merely a conjecture. Against the theory of a damaged MS. two points must be weighed : (i) the damage must have been done before any copy had been taken, and had it been done in St. Peter's lifetime, he would have written anew the destroyed portion ; (ii) a papyrus was rolled with the beginning outwards, so that the first chapter would be more likely to suffer accidental injury than the last. On the whole, therefore, it seems more probable that St. Mark, like many another author, died with his work unfinished. Anyhow, what we may take as quite certain is that the ending given in our Bibles, after verse

[1] They are of the fourth or fifth century.

8 of chapter xvi, did not form part of the original Gospel.

III

As we take a preliminary glance through the Gospel itself, we may notice how its character seems to confirm those traditions about its sources and aim which we have been examining.

We observed the belief of the early Church that St. Mark found his chief source in the " Memoirs of St. Peter." Now, as we look through the pages of his book, we see that he makes the call of Peter to discipleship almost his starting-point. There is not a word about the birth or youth of our Lord. The first verse is probably an editorial note by a copyist. The next two are a quotation from Isaiah. Then, in a most meagre fashion, all the stories of the Baptist's preaching, of our Lord's baptism, and of the temptation in the wilderness, are compressed into twelve short verses ! But after that comes the call of Peter, and the detailed narrative begins. We are told about Simon Peter's home, and his mother-in-law ; the disciples are described as " Simon and they that were with him."

(i. 36). The language is often that of an eye-witness when only the Twelve were with the Master. How unintentionally, too, the touching humility of the aged Apostle is revealed! He suppresses the high eulogy he received from Christ, " Blessed art thou, Simon," recorded in the Matthæan Gospel. But he insists that the scathing rebuke, " Get thee behind me, Satan," shall be made known to his hearers —and St. Mark could be sure of his wish that it should reappear in the written Gospel also.

Let us pass to another feature of this Gospel which must impress us at once when we turn over its pages. It seems to allot a quite disproportionate quantity of its space to the story of our Lord's Passion. St. Mark has to record the ministry of three years. Yet he assigns more than a third of his total space to describing the events of one week. Of course, we have to remember that his book is incomplete. We cannot tell to what length he carried it or proposed to carry it. But even when we take this into account, the contrast between the brevity of the earlier narratives and the detail with which the story of Holy Week is told seems remarkable.

We can understand it, however, if we accept the ancient tradition that for this part of his Gospel the writer was able to draw upon his personal knowledge. Why does he record the incident of the " certain young man "— i.e. a young man whose name he could give if he chose—that fled naked from the Garden of Gethsemane ? In itself it seems pointless. But its introduction is intelligible enough if that " certain young man " were, as tradition affirms, the Evangelist himself.

Another feature of the Gospel becomes evident at a first glance through its pages. It was intended for non-Jewish readers. Aramaic terms are interpreted. Jewish customs and seasons are explained, and only for Gentiles could such explanations be necessary. Again, the writer is evidently far more anxious to record what Jesus Christ did than what He said. The Sermon on the Mount is not included, or any such discourses as are found in the Fourth Gospel. There are only eight parables, as contrasted with twenty in Matthew and twenty-five in Luke. The Romans were far more interested in deeds than in words. The allegorical, mystical, and spiritual teaching would appeal enormously to Eastern people, but not to Western, and so the contents of St. Mark's Gospel accord with the tradition of its Roman origin.   The best means, St. Mark felt, of countering the slanders about Christianity which Nero had circulated was to set down a simple, truthful, and vivid account of Christianity's Founder, to show what kind of life He lived and what His deeds were during the years of His public ministry.   He would dwell specially on the last week, in order to show that the charge of treason against Rome was entirely unfounded, and that it was altogether the spite of the religious leaders in Jerusalem which brought Jesus to the Cross.

St. Mark's style fits his theme.   Even in a translation we can realize that it is simple, straightforward, and brisk.   It has movement and colour.   A Greek word variously rendered " forthwith," " immediately," and " straightway " is used more that forty times.   And St. Peter's memory was stored with many little details, lacking in the other Gospels, which are faithfully reproduced in Mark.   When, to take one example from many, the five thousand people are fed, Mark tells us that they sat down in ranks upon the green grass. In a way the English version cannot quite reproduce, that sentence gives us the vivid impression left on an eye-witness of the scene. " Green " serves to fix the season ; only in the spring-time was the soil of the plain green with growth. And the word rendered " ranks " means literally a herb-garden. There, then, is the picture : the wide expanse clothed in its spring-time green, and the multitude ranged in orderly rows upon it, looking like vast beds of herbs planted in lines at equal intervals. It is a picturesque simile such as no one inventing the story could have used. It is a vivid little bit of word-painting from memory, given by St. Peter to the Evangelist, and by him imbedded in his Gospel.

IV

Now we can take up this Gospel to read it through, understanding what kind of book it is ; a chronicle chiefly of our Lord's life and deeds, with outlines of His teaching, through the three years of His ministry ; a book derived principally from the reminiscences of St. Peter, but amplified by extracts from other documents and, towards the close, by the writer's own experience ; a book written at Rome, and designed for non-Jewish readers in the western world.   To keep those points in mind will enable us to read Mark with far more understanding and appreciation than otherwise would be possible.

I

In a far greater degree than any of the other Evangelists, St. Mark arranged his Gospel according to a definite plan. He divided it into two main sections, linked by a brief summary of intervening events, and prefaced by an introduction. " I must begin," we may imagine him to have said, " with some mention of John's ministry and our Lord's baptism and temptation. I have little information about that time, and none about any work the Master did in Jerusalem before going north to Galilee. But once the Galilean ministry is reached, I have plenty of material in my notes of Simon Peter's teaching. So, from the first day of his discipleship, I shall be able to give a fairly full account of what happened. One digression I must allow myself, because I want to insert the story of the Baptist's death. Otherwise I shall carry forward the narrative

5

without interruption.   I am fairly confident
that I have managed to arrange the events
in their right chronological order.   That
will enable me to show clearly the different
stages of the work in Galilee, and the causes
which forced our Lord to change His
methods.   Another main section of my book
will deal with the week of the Crucifixion.
This I can describe in detail from day to day,
for I have my own recollections of it, as well
as Simon Peter's.   But between the two
main sections, between the departure from
Galilee and the final entry into Jerusalem,
I have to interpose some account of a period
about which my information is scanty.   I do
know that during it our Lord preached in
Judæa and Peræa.   And I have documents
describing events which seem to belong to
this period.   From them I can choose a few
of the most important, without trying to
indicate the precise time or place at which
they occurred.   However, this intermediate
part of my Gospel shall be quite short, in
order that I may have ample space for the
story of the Crucifixion week.   Then I shall
describe the Resurrection "—and here we
can imagine St. Mark's design no further.
For, as has been said above, we do not know

at what length he proposed to tell the story
of the Resurrection.   What we do know is
that his account of it, as we now have his
Gospel, is broken off almost at the beginning.

At this point I will ask my reader to turn
to St. Mark's Gospel.   (I hope he possesses a
Bible printed in good legible type, and the
pages of which lie open easily !)   Let us look
at the different sections in Mark.   The
Introduction consists of the first fifteen verses
of chapter i.   Then the first main section,
describing the Galilean ministry, extends from
i. 16 to the end of chapter ix.   There follows
the short intermediate section, chapter x.
Its first verse describes a period extending
probably through some months.   Then we
have very short accounts of about half a
dozen incidents, that happened at various
times and at unnamed places within that
period.   With verse 32 the final journey to
Jerusalem begins.   So we come to the other
main section of the book—from xi. 1 to
xvi.   8.   Here we have a day-by-day
journal from Palm Sunday to Good Friday,
filling no fewer than five chapters, xi–xv.
Finally, St. Mark's account of the Resurrection begins with chapter xvi, is cut short

after eight verses, and verses 9–20 are the work of another hand.

II

The Introduction gives us one graphic detail that we do not get from any other source. When our Lord at the time of the temptation was in the wilderness, " he was with the wild beasts," it says. Otherwise the introductory fifteen verses need not detain us. The events of which they speak are put before us far better in the other Gospels. So we will pass on at once to the first main section—the story of Christ's ministry in Galilee. Most people will find it useful, I think, if at this point they will reread that section—chapter i. 16 to the end of chapter ix. I should like them to read it, for the purpose I have in mind, attentively indeed, yet rapidly, going through the whole section at one sitting. I would have them read it, on this occasion, without pause to meditate on any passage that seems specially suggestive or to elucidate any that seems difficult. To these a return can be made afterwards ; a few such points will be dealt with in the rest of this chapter. But what I want now is that the reader, by going quickly through the whole story in this way, should allow the cumulative effect of it all to make its full impression upon him. The wonderful effect of the whole never reaches us so long as we read a long and connected part of a book in small snippets.

Now, if I may assume the reader to have made this experiment, he will feel afresh, I think, the terse vigour of St. Mark's style, and his skill in showing how each stage of our Lord's work in Galilee was the natural outcome of the one before it. First, He teaches as a rabbi in the synagogues, and with immense success. His fame spreads, and increasing crowds throng to hear Him. His words, and His deeds of healing, create an amazement that St. Mark pictures most vividly. " What is this ? A new teaching ! " (i. 27, R.V.) is the word that runs round the synagogue at Capernaum. As yet there is no hint of opposition, even though He heals on the Sabbath. On the contrary, He is welcomed everywhere in the synagogues, " and he went into their synagogues through-out all Galilee, preaching and casting out devils " (i. 39). That is the first stage.

It does not last long. Soon the local religious leaders grow jealous of His immense hold on the people, while His doctrine and deeds seemed at variance with all their traditions. Notice how subtly St. Mark indicates the growth of this opposition. When first we hear of it, the scribes " reason in their hearts " (ii. 6) against Jesus, but do not venture to speak their thoughts aloud. Next, while they are still afraid to challenge Him directly, they make their criticism through the disciples (ii. 16). Then they criticize the disciples to Him (ii. 18, 24). After this they watch Him in the synagogue, to see if He will heal on the Sabbath, " that they might accuse Him " (iii. 2). Having drawn upon themselves His angry rebuke, they combine with " the Herodians " (iii. 6) —an ecclesiastical-political alliance—in trying to find means of destroying Him.

But it was not altogether of their own accord that the scribes in Galilee turned against our Lord. A powerful influence from the south was brought to bear upon them. Observe how skilfully, and incidentally, as it were, St. Mark indicates this. He does not tell us at length that reports about the dangerous new teacher were carried to Jerusalem, and that the Temple authorities, greatly perturbed, determined to send some of their scribes to Galilee in order to denounce the heretic and neutralize any influence He had gained.   Yet all that is implicit in his narrative when he tells how " the scribes which came down from Jerusalem said, He hath Beelzebub " (iii. 22).

What followed ?   Two results : first, that the hostility of the religious leaders closed the synagogues to Jesus.   Therefore, He has henceforth to give His teaching in the open air, and does that mostly on the shore of the Sea of Galilee.   And He orders " a little boat to wait on him " (iii. 9).   Partly that enabled Him to escape the actual pressure of the crowd, but it had another advantage also.   For the other result arising from the political hostility shown by Herod and his followers was that life in Galilee became increasingly dangerous for our Lord.   If there were a menace of arrest, He and the disciples could escape in the boat to the other side of the lake, where the jurisdiction of Herod Antipas did not run.

The synagogue-preaching was the first stage of the Galilean ministry, the open-air preaching the second. But the latter seemed unsatisfactory if the message were to be rightly understood and perpetuated ; a very small proportion of the " seed," as Christ said, fell on " good ground." So the third stage was reached. Instead of trying to teach many people a little, the Master sets Himself to teach a few thoroughly, in order that afterwards they may be able to transmit what they have heard. Increasingly He withdraws Himself from the multitudes, and, when He does meet them, speaks to them in parables the inner meaning of which is explained to the disciples alone. Towards the end, when Jesus passes through Gililee, " he would not that any man should know it " (ix. 30). Only when He has finished the Galilean ministry " multitudes come together unto him again ; and, as he was wont, he taught them again " (x. 1).

Now, the way in which St. Mark makes these stages reveal themselves to the careful reader, the deft touches by which he indicates them, the feeling he gives that each follows in inevitable sequence the one before it, the manner in which he compresses and subordinates details that do not directly help forward his narrative—all this seems a triumph of literary art. There has always been a tendency to underrate Mark in com-

parison with the other Gospels, because it
seems so succinct and matter-of-fact. In
truth, here is the art which conceals artifice.
Each Gospel has its own special merits ; each
contributes something to us which the others
lack. But neither of the other synoptic
Gospels can rival Mark as a narrative. In
Matthew the materials are grouped according to subject rather than set forth in
chronological order. Luke is rich in treasures
that we find in no other Gospel. Its author
excelled as a descriptive writer, and in his
Acts, after the first few chapters, he had
direct information and personal knowledge
which enabled him to write a connected
narrative without difficulty. It was otherwise with his Gospel. Probably he had far
more documents to work from than were at
St. Mark's disposal. The difficulty of col-
lating them and assigning each of the various
events described by them to its right place
and time must have been great. And St.
Luke had not, like St. Mark, intimate
memories of St. Peter's discourses to guide
him. Great, too, as were his own gifts, he
had not that genius for setting down facts
in their right order which distinguished St.
Mark. That he did attempt to arrange them

" in order " his preface bears witness. But he failed where St. Mark succeeded. When, as happens often, the chronology of Luke differs from that of Mark, we may be fairly sure that the order in Mark is the right one.

Even where there is no doubt concerning chronological sequence, the writer of history knows how hard is the task of handling the material in precisely the right way, of deciding what to omit, of writing so that the chief points, without undue emphasis, make themselves clear. He knows also that, in proportion as he succeeds, what he has done with such skill will seem to the casual reader a simple piece of straightforward narrative, requiring no skill at all. That, until we trouble to look closely, is the kind of effect produced on us by Mark. But if anyone with a literary sense, and, in particular, anyone who has ever tried to write history, will examine with care the story of the Galilean ministry as St. Mark wrote it, will notice the effects he gains, and the means by which he gains them, he will be deeply impressed, I am confident, by the technical skill of this work.

III

Let us look at it a little more closely.
Obviously, even if St. Mark had known what
had happened on each day, he could not
find space to record it all.   Sometimes he
must compress weeks or months into a
sentence.   Yet, that we may realize what
the working-life of Jesus in Galilee was like,
now and again he will spare space to describing a day in full.   He does that at the very
start.   That we may begin with a clear idea
of the ministry, he takes its opening day, a
Sabbath at Capernaum, and tells us all that
happened in it.   (The narrative begins at
chapter i. 21.)   Jesus enters the synagogue
at the accustomed hour of public worship—
usually 9 a.m.   After the prayers and the
readings from the Law and the Prophets, the
ruler of the synagogue turns to Jesus, as a
visiting rabbi, and invites Him to speak.
St. Mark does not pause even to summarize
the sermon ; that is alien to his purpose, it
would be a digression weakening the special
effect he wants to produce.   What he does
record is the astonishment it stirs in its
hearers.   Suddenly there is a disturbance in
the synagogue.   A man stricken with mania

struggles and screams. Jesus heals him, and the wonder of the gathering in the synagogue increases. They go to their homes, some in Capernaum, some in the neighbouring villages, full of excitement, and spreading everywhere the news of what they have heard and seen. By this time it is almost noon. Jesus, with Peter and Andrew, James and John, depart to their house for the midday meal. They find the household in dismay. Peter's mother-in-law has been stricken suddenly with fever. " Straightway " they tell Jesus. He goes to her room, takes her hand in His, and heals her. She is not merely brought to convalescence ; so immediate and complete is the cure that she rises from the bed in her usual health and " ministers to them," seeing to the delayed meal. The afternoon is spent in the enjoined Sabbath-day quiet. But the Sabbath ends at 6 p.m. No sooner is it over than " all the city was gathered together at the door," bringing " all that were sick and them that were possessed with devils." Into the shrill excited tumult of that Eastern crowd, amid the groans of the sick, the cries of the possessed, Jesus steps forth, and heals, and teaches.

After such a morning and evening a long night's rest must have been needed. Yet Jesus could not forgo that solitary open-air communing with His Father which was the mainstay of His life and work. So "in the morning, a great while before day, he rose up and went out, and departed into a desert place, and there prayed." It must have been Simon Peter who heard Him go, and, long years afterwards, told of that time in the hearing of St. Mark. At the outset of his Gospel, then, the Evangelist gives us this wonderful picture of a day in the life of Jesus—the first day of His public ministry, which so many others were like. Having given us one complete day to illustrate the synagogue-preaching period, St. Mark later adds a companion picture of a complete day in the period of open-air preaching. The reader will find it in chapter vi. 30–55. The Twelve, returning from their mission, find Jesus at work on the sea-shore. There is a huge crowd, of so many with eager questions, so many waiting to be healed, "that they had no leisure so much as to eat." He plans to go with His disciples "apart into a desert place" on the other side of the lake. They embark for this purpose. But there is little wind, and the crossing is slow—so slow that the people, seeing what He intends, can hurry round by land to the other side and get there first. When the boat touches shore, instead of the solitude on which He had counted, Jesus finds the same crowd that He had left behind! Instead of showing annoyance, He " had compassion on them," and, having taught through the morning and had no leisure for food, again " He began to teach them many things," until the day is " far spent." Then He uses His power to feed them. The disciples are sent back in the boat. Alone at last, " He departed into the mountain to pray." The night falls, but it is the time of the Paschal full moon. Presently He sees the disciples still on the lake, and " distressed in rowing, for the wind was contrary." And so " about the fourth watch of the night he cometh to them "—that is, about 3 a.m. ! Such is the record of another day's work.

Notice an example of St. Mark's dexterity of arrangement. In chapter vi. 7–13 we hear how our Lord sends forth the Twelve.

Their work is summarized in a couple of sentences. We hear no more of them until their return. If, however, that return were described in the next sentence, the interval of time would be difficult to realize. Accordingly, having mentioned the departure of the twelve, St. Mark chooses this point in which to insert the story of the Baptist's death. So our thoughts are taken to another theme, and it is with the desired feeling of time having passed that we hear, sixteen verses farther on, of the Apostles' return, when they told Him " all things, whatsoever they had done and whatsoever they had taught."

Enough has been said, I hope, to indicate the subtle skill in the writing of this Gospel, which at a first glance seems a wholly artless chronicle of events. And indeed it is only when we look closely at its construction that we begin to understand the book. There are no signposts on the road such as a modern writer would put up for our guidance. We do not find verses 21–36 of the first chapter introduced by the words : " here is an account of one day's ministry in Capernaum," or, later on, a sentence pointing out that at this stage

our Lord changed His methods. We are
left to note these things for ourselves. It
follows, therefore, that rightly to appreciate
Mark, we must read it with alert attention.

IV

One of the most valuable characteristics
of the book is its pellucid candour. St.
Mark is not afraid to attribute human
emotions and limitations to our Lord;
He feels grief, anger, surprise, amazement,
fatigue ; He asks questions for information ;
at times He is unable to accomplish what
He wills. Such phrases, remarkable in
themselves, become yet more striking when
we find that all of them are either toned
down or omitted entirely in the parallel
passages of the Matthæan Gospel. The
compiler of that Gospel was obviously
afraid that such sayings might be misunderstood, and be used to impugn our
Lord's divinity. Thus again the question
recorded in Mark " Why callest thou me
good ? " is most significantly transmuted
by Matthew into " Why askest thou me
concerning that which is good ? " (Mk. x.
18 ; Matt. xix. 17), where we cannot doubt
that Mark gives us the true form. The real

emphasis in it, of course, falls upon the adjective, not the pronoun; not "why callest thou *me* good?" but "why callest thou me 'good'?" It is the story of a man in a hurry, who comes "running" to Jesus and asks, "Good teacher, what am I to do to gain eternal life?" "First measure your words," is the answer. "You call me 'good.' You use that word lightly; what meaning has it for you? What is your standard of goodness—what your ideal? The divine one of perfection, for God only is truly 'good,' or the human conventional standard of your day? Begin by adjusting your moral values, by pausing to think what 'goodness' means." The writer of Matthew, however, fearing that the saying might be misinterpreted—as, indeed, it has been often—was afraid to record it with the candour of St. Mark.

Yet, for all its frank and eager insistence on our Lord's humanity, Mark insists no less that, in a unique sense, He is divine. It emphasizes His supernatural powers. It gives us the story of the Transfiguration. And it records the decisive answer of our Lord Himself: "Again the high priest asked him, and saith unto him, Art thou

6

the Christ, the Son of the Blessed ? And
Jesus said, I am." (xiv. 62). It is worth
while to notice that in this, the earliest
of our Gospels, the claim of Jesus to be the
divine Messiah is made quite explicitly ;
implicitly also it is the basis upon which
His unique " authority," both as a teacher
and a healer, is based.

Special emphasis in the story of His
Galilean work is laid upon His authority
over evil spirits, which He banishes from
their victims. " Preaching and casting out
devils " is a phrase in which St. Mark
summarizes His work (i. 39). So, too,
when the Apostles were sent forth " they
cast out many devils " (vi. 13). The
belief that many forms of illness were due
to evil spirits was held by all the people
among whom our Lord lived. That many
of such maladies were in truth due to quite
other causes is indubitable. That there
were no genuine cases of demoniacal
possession—or, indeed, that no such cases
exist to-day—is an assertion to which few
medical men who have worked among
primitive races would care to commit
themselves. But the important point for
us to remember as we read the Gospels

is that our Lord spoke and worked in accordance with the thought of His day. Dr. Headlam has put this admirably : [1]

" Our Lord's language is completely in accordance with the religious and scientific ideas of His contemporaries. He acts, recognizing fully what both the onlookers and those whom He cured would think. It is obvious that nothing else would have been possible on His part. Let us ask those who feel troubled by this what particular theory our Lord should have substituted for that current in His time. Do they think that He ought to have talked in the scientific and medical language of the present day ? It is obvious that to have done so would have conveyed no meaning to anyone who heard Him, deprived Him of power and influence, made His actions vain and ineffectual. The one condition of being able to exercise his ministry as a man teaching men was that He should do it in accordance with the thought and ideas of the day."

Dr. Headlam writes that with special

[1] In his *Life and Teaching of Jesus Christ*, p. 187.

reference to the belief in evil spirits current in our Lord's age. But it is true of many other beliefs of that time ; beliefs which Jesus Christ, having taken our nature upon Him, adopted or shared. A great number of the difficulties people feel as they read the Gospels will vanish if they keep this truth in mind. To understand the Gospels, we have continually to remember for whom they were written, and what were the ideas and knowledge of those people to whom the words of Jesus were spoken.

V

From the story of the work in Galilee we must turn to the other main section of Mark. The last journey to Jerusalem begins at verse 32 of the intermediate chapter, x. Its first words are unutterably impressive. In one sentence they give us a picture we get in no other Gospel. To appreciate it, we must remember what had happened. Despite its wonderful incidental results, our Lord's mission so far had failed in regard to its great purpose. He had meant to work through the national church of His country. That plan had been begun with every prospect of success. But after

a while, and with steadily increasing bitter-
ness, the leaders of the Church had set
themselves to oppose Him. Then He had
taken to the method of itinerant preaching
among the people, and then to that of
concentrating His instruction upon the
Twelve. Now, even Galilee, though its
people were His enthusiastic followers,
had become territory where He was in
constant danger of arrest, owing to Herod's
hostility. In fact, it was the popular
devotion to Jesus which alarmed Herod
and his advisers, who lived in fear of a
political revolt and an attempt to make
a king of this new leader. Long before
He had been ostracized from the synagogues.
His gospel of a spiritual kingdom had been
misunderstood even by His friends. There
was no great national religious movement,
such as He had desired, which would lead
up to His acceptance as the Messiah. What
could He do ? He could retire into the
country east of Galilee and continue to
teach and heal there in safety. Yet this
would not forward His supreme aim. Or
He could publicly enter Jerusalem at the
time of the coming Passover in a way that
would assert His claim to be the Christ.

Jerusalem was the home of His bitterest enemies. To take this step must mean His death. But by His death He might establish His Kingdom, as He had failed to do by His life.

To face those tremendous issues Jesus had gone apart to meditate. His disciples, with other Galileans, are on the road to Jerusalem for the Passover. Suddenly Jesus appears and places Himself at their head. His resolve is fixed. His decision has been made. There is a new look on His face which fills those who see Him with wonder and awe. That is the picture which Mark brings before us. " And they were in the way, going up to Jerusalem, and Jesus was going before them ; and they were amazed, and they that followed were afraid." We may well be grateful that St. Peter's memory of this supreme moment should have been enshrined for us in the Gospel of St. Mark.

The five chapters that follow give us the day-by-day account of Holy Week : Sunday (xi. 1–11) ; Monday (xi. 12–19) ; Tuesday (xi. 20–xiii. 37) ; Wednesday (xiv. 1–11) ; Thursday (xiv. 12–52) and Friday (xiv. 53–xv. 47). Again I would urge the reader to go through these five chapters at a sitting, without lingering on details, in order to realize their full effect. Then, in a way impossible if we take but a little at a time, we become conscious of the dignity, the restraint, the vivid detail, the quiet yet overwhelming force of this narrative. If, in one sense, it is magnificently simple, in another it is simply magnificent. It carries conviction. Its numerous little life-like touches and its candour make us sure that these chapters are based upon accounts given by those who saw what here is described. Beyond all else, and above all range of human imagination, stands out the figure of Jesus Christ as He deals with all manner of people and questions, as He ministers to His disciples, as He prays, and suffers, and dies.

There are, of course, some discrepancies in the accounts of the different Gospels. We should have far more reason to doubt their general trustworthiness if we found what would seem like a contrived agreement on every minute point. Again, elaborate attempts have been made to explain away the fact that in xi. 35-37 our Lord bases an argument on the assumption that Psalm 110 is the work of David, whereas in all probability it belongs to a much later age. But as Jesus used the medical knowledge of His own time, so He adopted the Biblical scholarship of that period. His acceptance of them then does not bind His followers to accept them to-day. The same thought will help us when we meet, in another Gospel, His use of the story of Jonah.

A small point in xiv. 41 is worth noticing, because it may serve to illustrate the fresh light thrown on the New Testament within recent years by the discovery of papyri. These have revealed the fact that Greek of the kind used in the writing of the Gospels was the common language of the time. Thus, though St. Mark wrote at Rome, far more of his readers there would know Greek than Latin. The papyri that have been unearthed are letters, inscriptions, business documents of many kinds, and so forth. Very many words occur in them that were previously thought to be unknown outside the New Testament, and thus we often get new ideas as to the real meaning of such words.

Now let us look at xiv. 41 of Mark.

It contains a sentence spoken by our Lord as the traitor Judas entered Gethsemane. In our English Bible we read "it is enough; the hour is come; behold, the Son of man is betrayed into the hands of sinners." Now what is the force of the word—it is one word in Greek—here translated "it is enough"? The numerous receipts that have been found among the papyri show that it was the word used on them, as the equivalent, so to speak, of our "paid." Literally it means "he has it in full"; that is, "he has received his payment." This suggests a rendering of the sentence in Mark far more significant than the rather pointless "it is enough." Our Lord is speaking of Judas. "He has accepted the bribe; the hour is come; behold the Son of man is betrayed into the hands of sinners."

As we read the account of our Lord's trials and condemnation, we should have in mind their various stages, not all of which are mentioned in Mark. We shall remember them more easily if we tabulate them, thus:

A. The ecclesiastical trial, on the charge of blasphemy.

(1) Jesus is taken to the house of Annas.

(2) He is tried by the Sanhedrin, under the presidency of Caiaphas, and declared guilty. But the proceedings were technically irregular, because the Law decreed that formal meetings of the Sanhedrin could only be held between dawn and sunset. Therefore—

(3) At dawn the Sanhedrin meets formally and passes sentence of death. But it has no power to execute this. On the other hand, the Roman governor would not listen to a charge of blasphemy. So there follows :

B. The civil trial, on the charges of sedition and treason :

(1) Before Pilate.

(2) Pilate tries to remit the case to Herod.

(3) Final trial before Pilate, and sentence of death passed by him.

After the Wednesday night there was no rest for the divine Sufferer before the tomb.

VI

We have seen that the last twelve verses of chapter xvi represent an attempt, of the second century, to complete the unfinished or mutilated Gospel. Another and shorter ending, of about the same date, is found in some MSS. It runs thus :

" And all that had been commanded they reported briefly to the companions of Peter. And afterwards Jesus Himself appeared to them, and from the east to the west sent out by means of them the holy and incorruptible message of eternal salvation."

As we close this book, let me make a final suggestion. The reader has followed the plan, I assume, of going straight through the two main sections, and then has looked at them, with the preface, intermediate chapter, and epilogue, in some detail. Now, after a few days' interval, so that he may return to it with an unwearied mind, let him set aside a quiet hour for reading through at a sitting the whole of Mark, from beginning to end. That will help to fix in his memory the points he has noted.

But, more than that, it will give him an impression of the book as a whole. The Gospel of St. Mark will mean more to him than ever it did previously. It will glow with fresh beauty, interest, and significance. It will become a book that, in a new sense, he understands ; a book the treasures of which he can now count as his own.

I

THE title of each Gospel, as we find it in the New Testament to-day, does not come to us from the original document. It was prefixed by some copyist and, in its earliest form, consisted of two Greek words only: " according to Matthew "— or Mark, or Luke, or John. To describe a letter from St. Paul as " Paul's Epistle to " this or the other church would have seemed quite legitimate at that period, but no one would have spoken of " Matthew's Gospel." The idea of the copyist who wrote " according to Matthew " at the head of his papyrus was that there could be one Gospel only, the Gospel of Jesus Christ. The book he was about to transcribe contained the setting forth of that one Gospel according to an individual tradition.   Before long, " according to " was understood as ascribing authorship to the name which followed. At first, however, it did not imply necessarily that the book in its completed form was written by the teacher named, though it did imply that his teaching was contained in it.

A rough analogy may make the distinction clearer. Let us suppose that some modern writer wished to popularize Macaulay's view of English History, and that he put together a book for the purpose. We should expect its main feature to be long passages transcribed from Macaulay, supplemented by quotations from other historians, and perhaps from researches of the compiler himself. Having completed his book, obviously he could not label it on the cover " Macaulay's History of England." Yet he might very well entitle it " English History according to Macaulay." In the same kind of way, " according to Matthew " did not strictly mean " here follows a book written by Matthew," but " here follows the Gospel of Jesus Christ according to Matthew's presentment of it." The reference is to the originator of the tradition, not necessarily to its recorder. Of course they may be the same. No later hand seems to have edited Mark or

Luke ; here we have two Gospel traditions written down in their ultimate form by the men whose names they bear. The Fourth Gospel, on the contrary, seems to be explicitly compiled by an editor from earlier written memoirs of a disciple. " This," says the editor in speaking of him, " is the disciple which beareth witness of these things and wrote these things, and we know that his witness is true " (John xxi. 24).

Thus the book we are now to examine is the Gospel " according to the Matthæan tradition," and the two conclusions about it which almost all modern scholars accept is, first, that it is not written by St. Matthew, and, secondly, that it contains much which St. Matthew wrote.

II

Perhaps these statements need elucidation. Let us consider them in turn. Why is it most unlikely that the Gospel, as we possess it, was written by St. Matthew himself ? Through many centuries, indeed up to a time comparatively recent, his authorship of it was accepted without question. As we shall see, however, the belief arose from a misunderstanding for which it is easy to account. And we have ample cause for calling the Gospel Matthæan, for feeling confident that it embodies St. Matthew's tradition, even if we cannot think that the book as it now stands was his work. Whoever the author, one fact about his method is clear. When he described the events of our Lord's ministry, as distinguished from reports, of His teaching, this writer did not do so in his own words. Instead, he borrowed the narrative that had been given already in Mark.[1] Sometimes he reproduced the sentences exactly as they stood. More often he

[1] Here, as on later pages, I speak of Matthew or Luke " copying Mark," because the brevity of the phrase is convenient, and also because it is really applicable, whether (as most critics think) they had before them the actual Gospel of Mark, or (as I incline to believe) they copied, not from the Gospel, but from the earlier " Memoirs of St. Peter " which Mark wrote down and afterwards reproduced in his Gospel. These memoirs would be eagerly sought after by the early Church, and copied often. If they were only to be found in Mark's Gospel, that Gospel would have had a great vogue. In point of fact, it met with a neglect that has puzzled students. But Mark himself had no great status. His Gospel as such would not be prized highly if his "Memoirs of Peter " had already been circulated in a separate form.

treated them with great freedom, altering and rearranging them, and omitting phrases he thought injudicious. But that his narrative sections are copied and not original is beyond question.

Now, is it likely, is it even conceivable, that St. Matthew, being one of the Twelve, wishing to describe the ministry he had witnessed day by day, would not describe in his own words what he had seen, but would be content to reproduce a ready-made account from another man's book ?

Take another point. Mark, embodying the memoirs of St. Peter, reproduces many passages which describe quite frankly the misunderstandings and the failures of the Apostles. This splendid candour obviously dismayed the writer of Matthew. Therefore, whenever in his copying he came upon such a sentence, either he toned it down or omitted it entirely. Thus, in place of "they disputed one with another, who was the greatest " and the rebuke which follows (Mk. ix. 34), we find " the disciples came unto Jesus, saying, Who then is greatest in the kingdom of heaven ? " (Matt. xviii. 1). Instead of " they understood not the saying, and were afraid to ask him " (Mk. ix. 32),

we have "they were exceeding sorry"
(Matt. xvii. 23). Among the sentences
appearing in Mark, but deleted from the
corresponding passages in Matthew, are
"their heart was hardened," "they ques-
tioned among themselves what the rising
from the dead should mean," "they wist
not what to answer him," and a good many
others. Thinking them derogatory to the
repute of the Twelve, the writer of Matthew
expunged them from his Gospel.

This practice of his is familiar, of course,
to all commentators, and is duly noticed by
them. But I do not know that any of them
has considered its bearing upon the question
of authorship. Supposing that St. Matthew,
being one of the Twelve, had been willing
to take over for his own work St. Peter's
record of facts, I cannot believe that he
would have tampered with it for the sake
of putting himself and his fellow-Apostles
in a more favourable light. But I can
easily believe these alterations and omissions
to have been made by a later disciple, if
it were he who compiled the Matthæan
Gospel. He would do it because he was
jealous for the honour of the Apostles in
the Church, and thought that honour would

be diminished by, as it seemed to him, St. Peter's most injudicious candour. This seems another reason for thinking that the Gospel, in its present shape, was not written by St. Matthew the Apostle.

But if he did not write it, what part had he in it, and how came his name to be linked with it ?   The answer is supplied by Papias, that second-century bishop who, as we have seen already, is quoted by the historian Eusebius.   Papias affirmed that St. Matthew wrote down in Hebrew the *logia*, or Discourses, of our Lord.   By " Hebrew " Papias doubtless meant " Aramaic," which was the vernacular in which most, if not all, of the Discourses had been spoken. Now the Discourses, of which the Sermon on the Mount is a notable example, form a very important part of the Matthæan Gospel.   None of the other synoptic Gospels record them with anything like the same completeness.   So we can easily see how the belief would arise that the reference of Papias was to the Gospel, and that he definitely named St. Matthew as the Gospel's writer.   That belief would be more readily encouraged because the theory that it came from an Apostle would invest the book with special authority. " This book is full of the Discourses ; Papias tells us that St. Matthew wrote down the Discourses ; therefore he must mean that St. Matthew wrote this Gospel." That was the line of reasoning, and, in an uncritical age, it was speedily accepted.

Yet it was mistaken. It ignored the fact that Papias and the other early witnesses quoted by Eusebius carefully state that St. Matthew wrote in Hebrew. But Matthew is written in Greek, and always was so written. Its narrative sections could not have been written in Greek, translated into Hebrew or Aramaic, translated back again into Greek, and still have kept just the same Greek wording that is found in Mark. It is possible, of course, that St. Matthew did write a complete Aramaic Gospel which has disappeared. But there is no evidence for that view. It is most unlikely that such a book written by such a man would have been allowed to pass completely out of sight. And Papias and the others do not affirm that St. Matthew made a Gospel. All that he did put down, according to them, was our Lord's Discourses.

That collection of Discourses, then, the compiler of the Matthæan Gospel took over, translated into Greek, and made them the most prominent part of his book. Because in this way so much of its value was due to St. Matthew's work, and because it enshrined his tradition, there was entire fitness in heading it at a later time with the words " according to Matthew." Then, as we have seen already, the compiler utilized, with his own characteristic modifications, the " Memoirs of St. Peter," either in their original form, or as reproduced in Mark. Thirdly, he had some independent sources of information. Thus his account of our Lord's Birth seems to have been derived from St. Joseph. Dr. Streeter conjectures a document he calls " M," originating from Jerusalem and coloured by the teaching of St. James, as another source of Matthew. But, without concerning himself with such intricate if interesting hypotheses, the reader will be on fairly sure ground if he believes the Gospel to be derived mainly from (*a*) the Discourses, (*b*) the Petrine Memoirs, and (*c*) private sources of information.

III

In order to read Matthew intelligently, we must keep in mind its point of view. We have noted already its main characteristic. Unlike Mark, which was intended for a Gentile public, Matthew was composed solely to meet the needs of the Jews. Its purpose was to show them Jesus as their King and promised Messiah. We can imagine the questions a Jew would ask when he was invited to accept Jesus of Nazareth as the Christ. Was He of the lineage of David ? Could it be shown that His needs accorded with those foretold of the Messiah by the prophets ? Was He a Conservative or a Liberal in the ecclesiastical controversies of His day ? Had He upheld the Law ? He had taught as a Rabbi ; what was His teaching ? How had He interpreted the traditions of the elders ? In particular, what were His views about the chief duties of religion, such as prayer, fasting, and almsgiving ? Apocalyptic writings, penned after the age of prophecy had closed, encouraged the people to expect the setting up of a divine Kingdom ; had Jesus proclaimed that Kingdom ? They had pictured a Day of Judgment, when God's chosen people would be vindicated and their enemies consumed. Had Jesus revived that hope ?

Such were questions a religious Jew would ask. Such were the questions Matthew was written to answer. And it was not intended only to convince doubters, but to strengthen the faith of Jews who already belonged to the Christian Church. It linked our Lord's life and teaching with the Scriptures they had been taught to venerate. And it combined, in a way that at times seems to us perplexing, the old belief in the exclusive privileges of the Jew with the new belief in a Church where there was neither circumcision nor uncircumcision. Some of the sayings are so reported as to have a distinctly Judaistic tinge : " I was not sent but unto the lost sheep of the house of Israel " ; " do not even the Gentiles the same ? " ; " after all these things do the Gentiles seek " ; " go not into any way of the Gentiles," with other sentences that seem to imply that Christianity is wholly Jewish. But in sharp contrast with these we find such sayings as " Many shall come from the east and the west, and shall sit down with

Abraham and Isaac and Jacob in the kingdom of heaven " ; " the kingdom of God shall be taken away from you and shall be given to a nation bringing forth the fruits thereof " ; " go ye therefore and make disciples of all the nations." These apparent divergencies may be present because the compiler has utilized a variety of sources coloured by different views. There can be no doubt, however, which strain of teaching was the more consonant with the ultimate intention of our Lord.

To understand the Matthew Gospel, then, we must always keep in mind the fact that it was intended, not for the world in general, but for Jewish readers. Its most probable date seems to be immediately before, or shortly after, the fall of Jerusalem in the year 70. On the whole, the latter seems the more likely. But the whole of this period must have been one of intense strain and doubt for the Jew. The Holy City was menaced if not already overthrown. That Second Coming, which the early Christian Church had looked for so eagerly and anticipated so confidently, was still delayed. Was the belief in Jesus as the Christ, after all, an illusion ? The old question of the

Baptist, " Art Thou He that should come, or
do we look for another ? " recurred with a
new intensity. To meet that question, to
allay those fears, the Gospel of Matthew was
written. Its author's endeavour was to
show that the life of Jesus was in such
precise accord with what had been foretold
of the Messiah that all doubts must be laid
aside.

We may feel that a book thus framed to
meet the special needs of Jews in the first
century cannot be the Gospel best suited to
the needs of Gentile readers in the twentieth.
And we may admit frankly that, if we judge
it from a purely modern standpoint, the book
has some evident flaws. We have noticed
already how its writer's fears about the
possible results of St. Peter's frankness led
him to omit some passages and to transform
others. The latter, at least, of these devices
is hard to justify. Again, he seems to stress
overmuch the predictive element in prophecy, while the way in which occasionally
he adapts a prophetic text in order to equip
an event with its prediction must seem
more ingenious than ingenuous. Perver-
sions of this type seem unjustifiable if we
regard them in the light of our own literary

ethics. But that is just what we have no
right to do. Undoubtedly the compiler of
Matthew altered and edited the documents
he cited in order to make them accord with
his ideas of fitness. Yet he would do that
with a perfectly clear conscience, for he was
but following the accepted practice of his
time.

Indeed, there is a true sense in which the
value of this Gospel is enhanced by the very
characteristics that seem most open to
criticism. Just in proportion as it is essentially Jewish in atmosphere, it does for us
what can be done by neither of the other
synoptic Gospels. Mark is a Gentile book.
Luke is a Gentile book. But our Lord spent
His earthly life as a Jew, in a Jewish setting.
Therefore it is Matthew, an essentially
Jewish Gospel, which helps us best to realize
that setting. Far more clearly than any
other it reveals the religious background of
our Lord's time, the creed and limitations of
those by whom He was surrounded, the
strength of the rabbinic tradition against
which He had to contend, His own work as a
Jewish religious teacher, and the professional
jealousy which brought about His death.
Remembering, too, that the book enriching

our knowledge in these ways is also the book which alone preserves for us in a complete form the Sermon on the Mount and the Lord's Prayer, certainly we shall not be likely to underrate the Gospel of Matthew.

I

EVEN a glance through the pages of the first two Gospels will show a striking point of difference between them. In effect, it is a difference of method due to a difference of purpose. We may attempt to state it concisely by saying that the aim of Mark is to tell a story, of Matthew to paint a picture. St. Mark's story, through no fault of his, is incomplete. There are periods in the ministry of our Lord concerning which he has little information. Then, in places of a consecutive narrative, his book becomes a record of detached incidents. He is sure that they are authentic, but his sources do not enable him to specify the exact time or place of their occurrence. When, on the other hand, his material is adequate, as it is for his descriptions of the Galilean ministry, and the last week in Jerusalem, he brings the scenes before us in accurate sequence. He is anxious to tell us not merely what happened, but when it happened. In fact, through this period, he is writing the story of our Lord's life.

The Matthæan editor follows quite another plan. The outline account of main facts he is content to borrow from Mark, reinforcing it by information from independent sources. Within this framework he arranges deeds and words, not according to their order of time, but their congruity of subject. It is easy to imagine him at work. He is, let us say, transcribing a parable. While he does that, he recalls another, rather similar in its moral. Down, therefore, it goes, immediately after the first. The one may have been spoken in Capernaum, the other two years later in Jerusalem. That does not trouble the compiler. Unlike St. Mark, he is not attempting to write history. For chronological order he cares very little. What he does care for is to set out our Lord's teaching in the clearest possible way. He shifts and transposes events into whatever sequence he thinks will best help his readers to grasp the teaching, and to gain a clear picture of the Divine Teacher, the Messiah of Israel.

It is very important, therefore, that we

should be prepared to find this system of grouping if we are to read Matthew intelligently. If we try to take it as a consecutive history, while having in our minds a fairly clear recollection of the Mark Gospel, we shall be hopelessly perplexed. We shall find repeatedly the same event described in both Gospels, but as happening, apparently, at quite different times. Elaborate efforts to " reconcile " the chronology of the two books have proved unconvincing. And well they might, the truth being that, except in outline, Matthew is not chronological at all.

Apart, too, from this aim of making his picture vivid by massed details, probably the compiler had a further reason for grouping. His book would be used for the instruction of Christian converts. Such teaching was given by the catechetical method, and it seems likely that the writer was himself a catechist. What he had to provide, then, was, as we should say, a book suitable for the use of study-circles. But these were study-circles learning by the oral method only ; it was impossible to equip each member of the class with a manuscript copy of the Gospel. That would be in the hands of the teacher alone. He would expound it, and repeat its most important passages until his hearers had memorized them. This they would be able to do with a rapidity that would astonish us. The training and development of the memory formed an essential part of Jewish education, and in early ages, before the invention of printing made reliance on it needless, verbal memory was much stronger than it is among civilized nations to-day.

Naturally, the writer would frame his Gospel with a view to the use it was to fulfil. He would so arrange its principal sections as to make the learning of them by heart as easy as possible. That may go far to explain his fondness for grouping. Consider, for instance, a number of sayings on kindred subjects spoken at various times during the three years' ministry. If they are all brought together and given consecutively, they will be memorized far more easily than if they appear at intervals, with long stretches of narrative between them.

Another device which Matthew seems to employ very often as an aid to memory is that of numbers. He puts together sayings or events in groups of three, five, or seven. In the Introduction to his *Commentary on Matthew* Dr. Plummer, who examined this characteristic closely, gave no fewer than thirty-eight " triplets " from the Gospel. That seems too large a number to be the result of accident. By way of example, let us take those found in a single chapter (xxiii) ; in it we have : Scribes, Pharisees, hypocrites ; feasts, synagogues, market-places (6) ; teacher, father, master (8–10) ; Temple and gold, altar and gift, heaven and throne (16–22) ; tithing of mint, dill, and cummin contrasted with judgment, mercy, and faith (23) ; tithing, straining, cleansing (23–26) ; prophets, wise men, scribes (34). The argument that the very numerous " triplets " in Matthew are intentional and a part of its scheme appears much stronger when we observe that, as Dr. Plummer pointed out, they are frequently absent from the corresponding passages in Mark and Luke. Often those Evangelists have two or four words where Matthew has the three. Thus Luke has " judgment and the love of God " instead of " judgment, mercy, and faith " ; he has " heart, soul, strength, and mind " where Matthew has " heart, soul, and mind."

Without insisting too much, however, on this detail of the scheme, we shall feel that the compiler of Matthew succeeded in his general purpose. His artificial rearrangement of his materials, if it lessened the value of the book as history, gave it both colour and precision. We should still find it much easier to learn by heart a chapter of Matthew than a chapter of Mark. This specially is true of the Discourses, which fill no less than three-quarters of the whole Gospel. Every reader wishing to strengthen his acquaintance with the most characteristic and valuable feature of the Matthæan Gospel should read the five great Discourses, each at a sitting. They are (1) the Sermon on the Mount (chapters v, vi, and vii) ; (2) the address on discipleship (x. 5–end) ; (3) the collection of parables (xiii. 3–53) ; (4) lessons of humility, renunciation, and forgiveness (xviii) ; and (5) the Apocalyptic Discourse (xxiv. 4–xxv. end). It is characteristic, again, of the compiler's orderly method that he rounds off each of these Discourses with the same formula, " when Jesus had finished " (vii. 28 ; xi. 1 ; xiii. 53 ; xix. 1 ; xxvi. 1). He will have no such ambiguity as occurs more than.

8

once in the Fourth Gospel, when it is difficult
to be sure at what point our Lord's words
end and the Evangelist's comment begins.

II

The Discourses, then, probably written
down by St. Matthew, and certainly translated, edited, and arranged by the compiler
of the Matthæan Gospel, form the largest
and most important part of the book. The
compiler was far more interested in them
than in the narrative of our Lord's life, and
frequently he abbreviated his other material
in order to give the Discourses at length.
More clearly than any of the others, this
Evangelist shows us Jesus Christ the
Teacher.

That was the guise in which He appeared
to His fellow-countrymen during the years
of His public work. At its outset He
" preached " for a short time, reiterating
the message of the Baptist. Occasionally
afterwards, as in the lament over Jerusalem,
His words must have recalled to their
hearers the language of the prophets. But
it was as a " Rabbi," a religious teacher,
that He was known and addressed, alike by
friends and enemies. As its equivalent, the

Greek word meaning " teacher " is used of Him repeatedly in the Gospels ; the Greek word which means " preacher " is not once applied to Him. That the ambiguous word " Master " should have been adopted by the English translators in place of " Teacher " is most unfortunate. Only in the margin of the Revised Version does " or, Teacher " appear as an alternative rendering. This undoubtedly has helped to conceal from English readers the fact which the Evangelists in general, and the editor of Matthew in particular, were anxious to make clear—the fact that Jesus lived and worked as a Teacher during most of His ministry.

The Jewish readers for whom the Matthæan Gospel was designed would recognize this fact at once. It would be shown by numerous little details, the force of which is apt to be hidden from us. For example, there seems little point to us in the statement that Jesus sat down, as in the verse prefacing the Sermon on the Mount. But it had ample point for a Jew. He knew that the ritual custom of a Rabbi was to stand for prayer and reading, and to sit down for teaching. When a Rabbi seated himself in public, it was a sign that he proposed to give instruction. Again, while anyone who chose might instruct about morals, Rabbis alone might expound the Law and the Tradition, giving directions about such matters as Sabbath observance. Not for a moment would the people have listened to a man presuming to handle such themes unless they had taken him for a Rabbi. Thus we can understand the immense astonishment of those who heard Jesus. He seemed to be a Rabbi, He spoke as one " having authority " to interpret the Law, " yet not as their Scribes " taught were the interpretations He gave! Only in the last week at Jerusalem, however, was His " authority " challenged.

So this Gospel helps us to realize an aspect of our Lord's life which, evident to early readers, has subsequently been obscured. It shows how, humanly speaking, He " rose from the ranks," beginning as an artisan, and becoming a recognized Teacher. That, perhaps, had been His ambition from early days, and therefore, because of its significance for His future, just one episode of His boyhood is recorded. St. Luke shows how in early boyhood already He wanted to be with the Rabbis, how eagerly He listened to their expositions. His Mother pondered these things in her heart, as mothers will, but there can have seemed little chance that the boyish wish would be realized. We can only guess at the self-denial, the hardly-won hours of study amid the work of an artisan that made possible its fulfilment. And how true to human nature is the story of that day when He returned to teach as a Rabbi in the synagogue of Nazareth ! Elsewhere He was honoured, but here, " Is not this the workman ? " His fellow-townsmen exclaimed, and were offended at Him. Matthew, in characteristic fashion, changes " the workman " into " the son of the workman," and tones down other phrases in the same story. We cannot doubt that Mark's is the true version.

" Workman," or, more precisely, " builder," seems a better rendering of the Greek word than the " carpenter " of our English Bible. The word, *tektôn*, does not occur elsewhere in the New Testament, but St. Paul describes himself as an *archi-tektôn* (whence our " architect "), which is translated " master-builder." *Tek-*

tôn was used often, but not exclusively, of workers in wood.[1] In late Greek it was used of a sculptor. And in Palestine the same man, when engaged in building, was often both carpenter and mason.[2] Certainly we shall find a new aptness in many of our Lord's sayings and illustrations if we may suppose that He worked as a builder before beginning His ministry as a Rabbi. He knew the importance of a good foundation, the difference between houses on rock and on sand. He himself would build His Church upon the rock. He knew the folly of the man who set out to build a tower without having obtained a precise estimate. To Him, as an expert, a disciple turned for an opinion on the great stones and buildings of the Temple. Finally, among the sayings attributed to Jesus in the Oxyrhynchus papyri is the sentence: "Raise the stone and there thou shalt find

---

[1] "It is worth while to remember that *tektôn* is wider than 'carpenter.'" Moulton-Milligan, *Vocab. of N.T. Greek*, p. 82. But cf. pp. 628, 629.

[2] Even though *tektôn* be rendered *faber tignarius*, the definition of Gaius (Dig. 50, 16, 235), "Fabros tignarios dicimus non eos duntaxat qui tigna dolarent, sed *omnes qui ædificarent*," should be remembered.

An excellent article on the whole subject, by Prof. F. Granger, appeared in the *Expositor*, June 1920.

Me ; cleave the wood and there am I."
The early date of these papyri, the fact
that most of the sentences they quote are
paralleled in the Gospels, and the very
striking character of this particular utter-
ance, seem to favour the possibility that
it may be authentic. At first sight, however, it appears to have a pantheistic meaning, difficult to reconcile with our Lord's
recorded doctrine. But the view of His
early years which we have been considering
may give the saying another and more
literal significance. " Raise the stone and
there thou shalt find Me ; cleave the wood
and there am I "—are these the words of
one Who has been both mason and carpenter,
one Who, in our everyday phrase, has put
Himself into His work ?

III

It is upon Jesus no longer the artisan
but the teacher that the Matthæan Gospel
fixes our gaze. Teaching as a Rabbi, it
would follow that He employed the rabbinic methods of teaching. If He did so, we
can be the surer that the record of His words
is trustworthy. Once more let us remind
ourselves that the Jews used different words

for " teaching " and " preaching " because they denoted quite different things. Preaching implied a connected discourse of some length. When Jesus preached (as He did in the Apocalyptic Discourse of xxiv–xxv), we cannot expect a verbatim report of all He said. The memory would not retain it or the Gospel contain it. Of the long Discourses, what we have must be an impression taken from the transcription, though doubtless the more striking phrases are set down as they were spoken. It is likely enough that St. Matthew, whose profession had accustomed him to the daily use of the pen, would commit his recollections to writing at an early date, and the trained memory of the Jew could achieve a fidelity of reproduction of which modern hearers would be incapable. Even so, however, we cannot have a full account of the preaching, or one in which misunderstanding may not occasionally have coloured a sentence.

It is otherwise with the teaching, and of this the Matthæan Gospel is mainly composed. What, for instance, we term " the Sermon on the Mount" was not, as we employ the word, a sermon at all. It is made up throughout of teaching, not preaching. The method of the Jewish religious teachers was to compress into a few succinct and pointed sentences the expression of any truth they deemed of special importance. Then the teacher would repeat the sentences many times with his disciples, until they knew them by heart. There is every reason to suppose that Jesus utilized this accustomed method of teaching by repetition. The pointed, gnomic sentences of which the Sermon on the Mount consists are exactly suited for this purpose. Again, the use of teaching by parable was common among the Rabbis ; a lesson so taught would easily be memorized. Here, too, our Lord found in vogue a practice exactly suited to His purpose. Hour by hour He would sit and teach until they who listened had His sayings firmly in their memories.

This makes it reasonable to believe that the Gospels preserve for us (with the change only of Aramaic into Greek) what Jesus actually said when He taught. Of the teaching, as distinct from the preaching, the reports given by the Evangelists do not read like summaries. We seem to have complete sentences, each of which leads

logically to the next. Yet a discourse
which, as we gather from the narrative, took
a considerable time for its delivery, can
often be read by us in a few minutes. The
fact is explained, however, if our Lord
followed the teaching method of His day,
repeating many times the same aphorisms
and parables, causing His pupils to recite
with Him His chief rules of conduct. Thus
taught, they would be able afterwards to
reproduce in writing the very words they
had heard. When we read the teaching in
the Gospels, we feel that we too are listening
to the authentic words of Christ. No
human being could have shaped mere
reminiscences of His doctrine into this
perfect form. If we can bring to our
reading not merely technical scholarship
but an alert literary sense, we must feel that
the Gospel record of the Discourses is
accurate. But we have no longer to
postulate some supernatural feat of memory
in order to account for this accuracy.

We can only guess at the toil which the
Master must have given, in those hardly-
won hours of solitude, to framing His
message. He had to condense its essence
into a few sentences. He had to enshrine

profound truths in phrases easily remembered by simple folk. We detract from His
greatness as a Teacher if we suppose Him to
have taught without long forethought. We
" multiply miracles beyond necessity " if we
imagine those matchless parables of His to
be mere improvisations. No ; our Lord knew
the true joy of the Teacher as He held the
attention of the listeners by some carefully-
planned lesson, as they recited with Him
the Beatitudes or His Prayer. He knew
the joy of the creative artist as He thought
out, in all its exquisite detail, the story of
the Prodigal Son.

IV

It is, then, its picture of our Lord as the
Teacher, and the detail in which it records
His teaching, that chiefly give this Gospel its
immense and enduring value. But there is
also much else in it both of historic interest
and practical instruction. In order to understand the book as a whole, however, the
reader must keep in mind its primary
object of convincing Jewish readers that our
Lord was the Messiah, the King for whose
advent they had been taught to look.
That purpose dominates the book from

beginning to end. The genealogy with which it opens is intended to show that Jesus is of the royal line, is legally descended from David. The story of the Magi is symbolical of homage to a King. Ten parables, given in this Gospel alone, are all parables of the divine Kingdom. At the very end of the Gospel the Risen Lord declares that " all authority hath been given unto Me in heaven and on earth." The book is pre-eminently the Gospel of the Kingdom.

Naturally enough, few modern readers trouble themselves to scrutinize the genealogy which prefaces the work. Yet it is worth looking at, as a curious example of the manner in which the compiler arranges his material with a view to its being easily memorized. The purpose of the genealogy is to show our Lord's descent from David, and " David " therefore is the keyword. As in other early alphabets, each Hebrew letter denoted a number. There are three letters in the Hebrew word David, and the sum of the figures of which they are the equivalents is fourteen. Accordingly, the table is artificially divided into three groups, and the appended note states : " So all the generations from Abraham unto

David are fourteen generations ; and from David unto the carrying away to Babylon fourteen generations ; and from the carrying away to Babylon unto the Christ fourteen generations." In point of fact, one name is missing from the third group, as it contains thirteen only. Reference to the Old Testament shows that there should have been eighteen names in the second group. Indeed, errors abound in the list. They would not seriously perturb its author. He had achieved his purpose, which was to provide a table of descent connecting our Lord with David, and to put it into a form which could be remembered.

The story of the Birth, as given in Matthew, seems, as we have noted already, to be derived from St. Joseph. Indeed, its information, if authentic, could hardly have come from any other source. And that it is authentic will probably be the feeling of most readers who study it without prepossessions. There is about it a straightforward simplicity, an apparent desire to set down the salient facts without a word of unnecessary comment or detail, that place it in striking contrast with stories of the miraculous Birth found in the apocryphal Gospels, abounding with fantastic portents. It will be better to postpone further consideration of the subject until we are looking at the account of it in Luke. The fact that we have not one narrative only of the Virgin Birth but two, derived from quite independent sources, has its own evident significance. In order to understand the Matthew narrative and to appreciate the action of St. Joseph, we ought to remember that betrothal was, among the Jews, a formal and legal act. As Deut. xxii. 23, 24, shows, unfaithfulness in a maiden after betrothal was punishable by the same capital penalty as unfaithfulness in a wife after marriage.

From the point of view of historical evidence, the inclusion of an episode in Luke is far more weighty than its appearance in Matthew. For St. Luke was a careful historian who, as he tells us, was at pains to examine his materials critically and to shape them into an accurate account. The editor of Matthew, on the contrary, was not a historian in this sense. He had fulfilled his purpose when he had painted his picture of Jesus as the Messiah, the fulfiller of prophecy, and had preserved for us those records of His teaching which St. Matthew had written in Aramaic. That, the main part of his book, is invaluable. In addition to it, and the outline adapted from the Mark sources, he gives us occasionally some piece of a tradition which has nothing like the same authority. As instances, we may take two stories which in themselves are puzzling. Both occur in Matthew only, and I think we may be relieved to find them only in this, the least historical of the Gospels.

One (xvii. 24–27) is of the way the Temple tax was paid. " Go thou to the sea," Peter is commanded, " and cast a hook and take up the fish that first cometh up ; and when thou hast opened his mouth, thou shalt find a shekel ; that take, and give unto them for me and thee." That command may have been given as the Matthæan Gospel records it ; obviously, no final proof is possible. But many of us must have felt rather disquieted by this story. It seems just the kind of miracle that Jesus did *not* work : a miracle for His own gain, and a miracle to obtain a few shillings that could have been provided in a normal way. It reads much more like the conventional tale of magic than a Gospel miracle. None of the other Gospels mention it, not even Mark—a fact the more

striking when we remember that Mark is
based on the "Memoirs of Peter." Even so
conservative a critic as Dr. Plummer
suggests that the words used by our Lord
may have been misunderstood or modified
in tradition. "'In the fish that thou
shalt catch thou shalt find what will pay for
me and thee' might mean that the fish would
sell for as much ; and this would easily take
the form which Matthew records."

The other is a strange portent immediately after the Crucifixion described by
Matthew only. All three Gospels state
that the veil of the Temple was rent.
Matthew adds that there was an earthquake,
" and the tombs were opened, and many
bodies of the saints that had fallen asleep
were raised ; and coming forth out of the
tombs after his Resurrection they entered
into the holy city and appeared unto
many." This very perplexing statement
is not even intelligible as it stands, for it
describes this rising from the tombs as
happening (*a*) at the time of the Crucifixion,
and (*b*) after our Lord's Resurrection. We
may feel sure that someone inserted the
words " after his resurrection " without
noticing the confusion they caused, but

anxious that Christ's priority as " the firstfruits of them that slept " should be preserved. Apart, however, from that detail, what can we make of the fact that St. Peter and St. Mark knew nothing of an event so stupendous ? For that they should have known of it, yet left it unrecorded, is unthinkable. St. Luke, again, either never met the story or deemed it unhistorical, and therefore unworthy a place in his Gospel. Anxious though St. Paul is to convince the Corinthians that the dead will be raised, he does not believe that already the bodies of " the saints " have come out of their tombs and have been seen by many in Jerusalem. In short, there seems ample ground for concluding that the editor of Matthew, who did not scrutinize and examine his material like St. Luke and had not the first-hand evidence which came to St. Mark from St. Peter, has here allowed a legend to find a place in his narrative. I think that very many readers will be glad that this view can be taken, not as an arbitrary escape from a difficulty, but as a reasoned conclusion with real evidence to justify it.

But the most mysterious passages in

9

Matthew are, beyond doubt, the great
Apocalyptic Discourse of our Lord
recorded in chapters xxiv and xxv. Much
of it is found in Mark and Luke also, but
Matthew's is by far the fullest version.
Strikingly enough, there is none of this
apocalyptic in the Fourth Gospel; here it
is to the coming of the Holy Spirit, not to
the return of Christ, that the disciples are
to look forward. In the synoptic Gospels,
and in Matthew particularly, predictions
of an ultimate day of judgment are mingled
with predictions about the siege and
destruction of Jerusalem. That the words
recorded as spoken by our Lord deal with
both these themes, not one only, seems
incontestable. Some of the sentences refer
in a most explicit way to the attack on
Jerusalem, but others cannot possibly, as
they stand, be limited to that event. It is
a world-judgment, with the return of Jesus
in glory, that these foretell. That the
Church in its first years expected that final
return and judgment to be almost immediate
is a fact of historical certainty. We find
it quite clearly, for example, in St. Paul's
first letter to the Thessalonian Church.
The belief cannot have been derived from

the Gospels in their present form, because
1 Thessalonians is earlier in date than
Mark. On the other hand, the writers of
the Gospels may have been influenced by
the existing belief. That would make them
tend, almost unconsciously, to interpret
general sayings of our Lord in a particular
way, and to give some words a stress and
special application which were not in the
mind of their Speaker.

Apart from mere surmise, however, we
ought to remember when reading the
Apocalyptic Discourse in Matthew how
greatly the religious Jews had been
influenced by earlier apocalyptic writings.
In mysterious and poetic language they had
made familiar many ideas which recur
in the Gospels. When, for instance, we
examine the Book of Enoch, the latest
parts of which seem to have been written
at least half a century before the birth of
Christ, and compare its picture of a judg-
ment-day with that given in Matthew, we
shall be impressed by the resemblance.
Here is a part of the Matthæan picture
(xxv. 31, etc.) :

" But when the Son of man shall come

in his glory, and all the angels with him,
then shall he sit on the throne of his glory :
and before him shall be gathered all the
nations : and he shall separate them one
from another, as the shepherd separateth
the sheep from the goats : and he shall
set the sheep on his right hand and the
goats on the left. . . . And these shall
go away into eternal punishment ; but the
righteous into eternal life."

And here an extract from the Book of
Enoch :

" And the Lord of spirits seated him
on the throne of his glory . . . and there
shall stand up in that day all the kings
and the mighty and the exalted and those
who hold the earth, and they shall see
and recognize how he sits on the throne
of his glory, and righteousness is judged
before him. . . . And one portion shall
look on the other, and they shall be terrified,
and they shall be downcast of countenance,
and pain shall seize them when they see
that Son of man sitting on the throne of
his glory. And he will deliver them to the
angels for punishment, to execute judgment

on them because they have oppressed his
people and his elect. . . . And the righteous
and the elect shall be saved in that day,
and they shall never thenceforward see the
face of sinners and the unrighteous, and
the Lord of spirits will abide over them,
and with that Son of man shall they eat
and lie down and rise up for ever and ever."

Did our Lord borrow the poetic imagery
of apocalyptic, with which His hearers
were familiar, for His own teaching ? Or
did the writer assimilate and group the
memories of this discourse so as to bring
them into line with apocalyptic ? That
also, when we remember his treatment
of prophecy, seems possible. Obviously,
all such points must remain uncertain.
What is clear, however, and what it is
important to remember, is the affinity
between earlier apocalyptic writings and
the teaching of our Lord, according to the
Matthæan Gospel, about the Last Judgment.
If we have that in mind, we shall not
repeat the common error of interpreting
the mystic language of Oriental symbolism
as though it were literal prose. The general
teaching is clear enough, but our desire

for precise knowledge, our tendency to say that this must mean exactly that, our attempts to fix " the day and the hour," despite explicit warning, must always be futile. It is not at all points that we shall ever be able to understand the Gospels, and we should admit the fact frankly. Such a book as Matthew, wholly designed for Jewish readers in the first century, must contain allusions and modes of expression to which we have lost the key. But there is a more profound reason also for the limitations of our knowledge. Much already we are allowed to know, and more will be revealed by future thought and research. Yet, because He is more than man, the Jesus of history must ever remain for us in some degree the Jesus of mystery too.

I

IF we were to be deprived of all but one
Gospel, what would our choice among
them be ? There are many people to
whom, especially when old age steals on,
the Fourth Gospel appeals beyond any
other. Problems of its origin do not
perturb them ; in its compelling influence
they find all the proof they need of its
authenticity. Its tranquil charm and deep
spiritual insight give it a unique place in
their affection. Among younger readers,
probably most would give the first place
to Luke. Of the three synoptic Gospels,
indeed, one may believe that an almost
unanimous verdict would adjudge Luke
to be the most beautiful. Here it is we
find the beloved Christmas picture of the
herald angels, of the shepherds at the
manger ; it is this which gives us our

Magnificat and Nunc Dimittis. We should have no parables of the Good Samaritan and the Prodigal Son, no picture of the walk on Easter evening to Emmaus, if we had no Luke. Apart, too, from details, the book as a whole has a charm of style not to be found in Mark or Matthew. Mark is a concise and vivid record of the essential facts, an historical record to which its early date and its direct link with St. Peter lend extreme importance. Matthew is the characteristic work of a Jewish scribe. But Luke has an individual note, a range of sympathy, a joyous appreciation of what is noble, that specially endear it to us. Perhaps Renan was not far wrong when he termed St. Luke's Gospel "the most beautiful book in the world."

Its author was a physician, an educated man writing for educated readers. We have observed that each Gospel was written at a special time to supply some definite need. It is not difficult to identify the circumstances which caused St. Luke to take his pen in hand. A stage in the growth of the Christian Church had been reached when it began to draw recruits from the aristocracy of the Roman Empire. Neither the somewhat crude writing of Mark nor the Judaistic exposition of Matthew would satisfy readers of this class. As Dr. Streeter has said,[1] " Once Christianity began to reach members of the high aristocracy, there would arise a new and insistent demand for a life of Christ which would not only jar less on the literary taste of educated circles, but would also make it clearer than does Mark that Christ was, and knew Himself to be, no mere Jewish Messiah, but a World-saviour, the founder of a world religion. The Third Gospel is an attempt, and an extraordinarily successful one, to meet this demand."

Side by side with this purpose must be set another. Those members of the upper classes who thought Christianity a mere Jewish superstition would not feel bound to oppose it actively so long as the great majority of its adherents were drawn from the proletariat. They would view it with disdain. But their animosity against it would become far more violent when some of their own friends and relations became

[1] *The Four Gospels*, p. 537.

its converts. Already there was a vague belief that the Church was a treasonable society, which held secret meetings in order to plot against the State. The Founder of this sect, it was said, had been crucified by the procurator of Judæa for inciting His fellow-countrymen to refuse tribute to Cæsar. Nero, for his own purposes, had encouraged the belief in Rome that the Christians were a league of criminals. Plainly, it was most important to refute slanders of that kind. In A.D. 80, which seems the most probable date of St. Luke's Gospel in its complete form, Nero had been dead for twelve years. The reign of Domitian, with its cult of emperor-worship and resulting persecution of the Church, was still ten years ahead. Meanwhile, whatever the official attitude, the Christian community seems to have been little molested. What attacks there were came merely from local officials. On the other hand, a number of aristocrats were joining the Church, and a much larger number were making interested enquiries about it. What was the true story of its origin ? How had its Founder lived and taught ? Was it merely a form of Judaism ? Was it tinged with treason

to Rome ? The demand for definite information on such points was reasonable
enough, and St. Luke set himself the task
of supplying it.

His first concern was to write accurate
history. He was anxious that Theophilus,
and many another like him, should be
reassured about the historical basis of
Christianity. His work should be one to
which they could turn with the knowledge
that the author had been at great pains in
examining and sifting his materials, and had
satisfied himself as to the trustworthiness
of all that he included in it. His preface
emphasizes the trouble he has taken to
make his book trustworthy. He has far
more sources of information to draw upon
than had St. Mark. He is far more critical
in choosing from this material than was the
editor of Matthew. Something has been
said in chapter ii (p. 38) of the sources at
his disposal. He feels he has utilized them
in a way to justify the claim that he has
set down everything " accurately " and
" in order." The second of these terms is,
in point of fact, less well deserved than the
first. St. Mark had written some fifteen
years earlier, and had the " Memoirs of St.

Peter " to guide him on points of chronology.
St. Luke's task in this respect was made the
more difficult by the large number of written
documents and other witnesses he con-
sulted. He could, and did, secure trustworthy accounts of what happened, but
to determine the precise point in the
ministry at which each happened was far
more difficult. He tried his best to arrange
them in due sequence, but with only
partial success.

Yet the exact occasion of an event
matters far less than that the account of
the event itself should be trustworthy, and
the minute scrutiny to which both the
Third Gospel and Acts have been sub-
jected within recent years has vindicated St. Luke's accuracy as an historian.
Primarily, then, he wrote his Gospel in
order that educated Roman citizens
should have in their hands a Life of
Christ on the strict veracity of which they
could rely.

With this purpose he combined another.
What he wrote was to serve not only as a
history of the Christian religion but a
defence of it. Both the Gospel and Acts
are planned to refute the allegation that

Christianity is a merely Jewish creed, and that from the first it was condemned by the officials of Rome. St. Luke does this most effectively by showing that our Lord addressed His message to Jew and Gentile alike, that it was a Jewish crowd which clamoured for His death, a Roman procurator who affirmed "Ye have brought unto me this man, as one that perverteth the people (i.e. incites them against Cæsar) : and behold, I, having examined him before you, found no fault in this man." More fully than any other Evangelist he records Pilate's repeated protestations of our Lord's innocence.

Then the reader should notice with what skill St. Luke carries out in his second volume the same purpose. He shows how the attacks on St. Paul came not from Rome, but from the Jews, how one Roman court after another—of Gallio, of Felix, of Festus—found him innocent ; how well-disposed to him were various Roman officials, from Sergius Paulus onwards ; how his transhipment to Rome came not from any condemnation by a Roman tribunal, but from his own action : " This man might have been set at liberty if he had

not appealed unto Cæsar." And at the
end, with this clue to his purpose, we shall
see that the last words of the book are no
tame casual sentence, but a triumphant
climax. "If this Christian teacher had
been regarded as a dangerous traitor by the
authorities at Rome, what would have
happened on his arrival there? He
would have been allowed to utter no word
of his mischievous doctrine. He would
have been flung into prison. His trial and
execution would have followed swiftly.
Such must have been the sequel if this
theory were true that in the first days
Rome condemned Christianity as treasonable. But what, in point of fact, did
happen? He abode two whole years in
his own hired dwelling, and received all
that went in unto him, preaching the
kingdom of God and teaching the things
concerning the Lord Jesus Christ with
all boldness, no man forbidding him."
Those are the last words of Acts, and
they are the culmination of the argument
implicit through St. Luke's two volumes.
To keep in mind that purpose of St.
Luke, and to notice the subtle skill
with which he accomplishes it, is a con-

siderable help towards understanding his writings.

II

Who was the " Theophilus " to whom both Gospel and Acts were dedicated ? That is a question we cannot answer with any confidence. Theophilus may have been a real name, but also, and perhaps more probably, it may have been a pseudonym veiling, for the sake of prudence, the identity of some Roman aristocrat. Whoever this " Theophilus " (meaning literally, " lover of God ") may have been, we may safely assume that he belonged to the aristocracy, the special class of readers for whom the Third Gospel was designed.

Another point of interest in the dedicatory preface—the first four verses of the first chapter—lies in the fact that it is written in " classical " Greek. Its style is an imitation of those stately opening sentences with which historians in long previous ages had begun their chronicles. The remainder of the book is written in the colloquial Greek of its own time, though, except when St. Luke is merely transcribing other documents, in a better style than the other Gospels.

But the construction of these prefatory sentences is formal and archaic. An imperfect analogy from modern literature may be used to illustrate the point. Among Mr. Kipling's earliest works was a small collection of stories called *In Black and White*. The stories are phrased in modern colloquial English. They are accompanied by a dedication, filling two pages, addressed to " My Most Deare Father," which opens thus :

" When I was in your House and we went abroade together, in the outskirtes of the Citie, among the Gentoo Wrestlours, you had poynted me how in all Emprysez he gooing forth flang backe alwaies a Word to hym that had instruct him in his Crafte. . . ."

—and so forth. The reader perceives at once that, while the stories are done in the English of the nineteenth century, this dedicatory letter is an imitation of the English of the sixteenth century. That is comparable to the difference between the preface and main body of the Third Gospel. A literary artifice of that kind would have no point for any but educated readers, and its use is a further proof that for educated readers St. Luke designed his work.

It has been suggested—and 'I think the evidence for this view is very strong—that Luke, as we now have it, is, to adopt modern phraseology, a " revised and enlarged edition," and that, after his original draft was finished, St. Luke acquired additional information which he wished to include in his book. Beyond anything else in importance among the fresh knowledge he had gained was the story of the Birth and Infancy. Therefore he now inserted it immediately after his preface, and it occupies the remainder of chapter i. and the whole of chapter ii. Originally, if this view be correct, the Gospel itself, after the preface, began with what is now chapter iii in our version :

" Now in the fifteenth year of the reign of Tiberius Cæsar, Pontius Pilate being governor of Judæa, and Herod being tetrarch of Galilee, and his brother Philip tetrarch of the region of Ituræa and Trachonitis, and Lysanias tetrarch of Abilene, in the high-priesthood of Annas and Caiaphas, the word of God came unto John . . .''

Certainly this, with its full and careful fixing of the period, does seem the kind of sentence with which an historian would begin his narrative, does read as though it had been designed as, apart from the preface, the first of his book. Of the Gospel of the Infancy something more will be said in my next chapter. Here we are considering only the main outlines and general character of the book.

III

What are the chief impressions it makes upon us as we look again through its pages ? We see at once that it contains a great number of parables, but we ought to note also that of the total, which is twenty-three, no fewer than eighteen are not recorded in any other Gospel. That helps us to estimate our debt to St. Luke, and it shows again what rich sources of information he had, in addition to those that had been used already in Mark and Matthew. Even when an incident recorded by him has been described by another Evangelist, we shall find that St. Luke often adds some phrase or detail that makes the picture more vivid and complete. As one small instance out of many, we may take the beginning of the story about the call of the fishermen-disciples : Mark and Matthew both mention only that Jesus was standing by the lake ; Luke (v. 1) has : " Now it came to pass, *while the multitude pressed upon him and heard the word of God*, that he was standing by the lake," etc. A late tradition affirmed that St. Luke was a painter, as well as a physician. We can neither prove nor disprove this statement, but at least no one who reads the Third Gospel and Acts with care can doubt that St. Luke was a most skilful painter in words.

Perhaps his work as a doctor in fœtid Oriental cities had helped to give him his keen sympathy with the poor. That is very evident in his Gospel. In recording the Master's words, St. Luke always chooses the tradition which lays most stress upon the moral dangers of wealth. Indeed, the contrasts in this respect between the Gospels of Matthew and Luke are very striking. Matthew's " Give to him that asketh of thee" becomes "Give to every one that asketh"; the Matthæan beatitude "Blessed are the poor in spirit" is "Blessed are ye poor" in Luke, with the addition "woe unto you that are rich!" Matthew gives "sell that thou hast" as the Master's teaching; Luke intensifies the saying into "sell all that thou hast." And in Luke alone we find the parables of the unjust steward, of the foolish rich man, of Dives and Lazarus.

Perhaps it was again his medical work, combined with his freedom, as a Gentile, from Jewish sex prejudice, which accounted for another well-marked feature of his Gospel. This is the place given in it to women— the first sign of the wholly new status in the world which was to be brought to women by Christianity. We feel that St. Luke is pre-eminently the right Evangelist to relate the story of the Birth from the Mother's point of view. And he individualizes women, as no other Evangelist does. He alone gives the names of the women who accompanied and ministered to our Lord. He alone gives us the domestic episode of Martha and Mary, that lifelong study of two contrasting feminine characters. How convincingly, yet in how few words, it is set before us ! The raising of the widow's son at Nain is a miracle recorded only in this Gospel. And that poignant detail of the Crucifixion story, the picture of the weeping " daughters of Jerusalem " who follow Jesus to Calvary, is one we should have missed had it not been for this Gospel of Luke.

Because in earlier years St. Luke was the close friend and travel-comrade of St. Paul, many scholars have attempted to identify in his Gospel the influence of the Pauline theology. All, or almost all, the parallels they try to establish seem fanciful. On one great principle, however, there is evident accord between St. Paul, the Hebrew of Hebrews who became the Apostle of the Gentiles, and St. Luke, the Evangelist eager to show that Jesus Christ was a light to lighten the Gentiles as well as the glory of Israel. The love of the Heavenly Father for all men, and for each individual sinner who repents ; the mission of the Son as the Saviour of all the world—these are the truths with which St. Luke's heart is full ; this is the message he wished his Gospel to bring to its readers. It does that still. We cannot turn its pages without being impressed by its charm, its humanity, its happiness. This is the kind of book which brings health to the soul in an age like ours. Its author is still a physician, and still beloved.

I

PROBABLY it is even more true of Luke than of Mark or Matthew that here it is a book we must read by fairly long sections at a time if we are to appreciate rightly its full power and charm. To do this is made easier by the well-marked divisions into which this Gospel falls. The first, as we have seen already, is the " Infancy " narrative of chapters i and ii. There is a special reason for studying them with alert attention. For nowadays the doctrine of our Lord's Virgin Birth is the theme of frequent discussion, and of discussion, especially in the popular press, that is not always well informed. Yet the evidence bearing on the question is accessible enough, and, very plainly, the issue is not one which interests technical scholars alone. Every one of us must be deeply concerned to know whether the statement of the creed that our Lord was born of a Virgin is, or is not, one that we can reasonably accept.

Absolute proof, either positive or negative, must be impossible, and it would be futile to contend that the historical evidence for the Virgin Birth is as strong as the evidence for the Resurrection. Yet we are bound to ask whether or no we are fairly entitled to retain the belief. We are bound to ask, as we finish the first two chapters of Luke, whether what we have read is fact or fiction. One or the other it must be. There is no middle term. Either our Lord's Birth was of the super-natural kind which St. Luke describes, or it was not.

St. Luke's own opinion is clear enough. As we read these chapters, the impression they give us is that the writer feels certain about the truth of his narrative. A historian, who was also a medical man, would not have immediately followed a preface guaranteeing his careful accuracy with the story of the Virgin Birth unless he had for it what seemed to him absolutely convincing evidence. We feel, too, how desperate an attempt to invalidate the story is that which depicts it as a pagan myth taken over by Christianity. We recall the intense dread of, and hostility to, paganism shown by St. Paul and the Church of the first century. We remember

St. Luke's close association with St. Paul. We think again of his preface. And we must feel that to be asked to believe that immediately after it this educated Christian historian began his Life of Jesus with an adaptation of a pagan myth is to be asked to believe the incredible.

Another point that will strike us as we read this narrative carefully is that, whatever the immediate source from which St. Luke derived it, it must have come originally, if it be true, from the Mother of our Lord. Some of its details could have been known to her only. We shall observe also that while the Luke story and the Matthew story are from different sources, the one from Mary's standpoint, the other from Joseph's, and while there is a consequent difference in the events which each selects for narration, there is yet no real inconsistency between them. Each tells part of the story of the Birth, but neither part contradicts the other. Another point brought home to us by a careful reading of St. Luke's first two chapters is that this Gentile writer has obtained most of them from a Jewish source. They abound with Jewish turns of speech. The Benedictus, Magnificat, and Nunc Dimittis are hymns written according to the rules of Hebrew poetry. We must not forget, indeed, that some scholars have attributed the Hebrew (or Aramaic) turns of speech in these chapters to the skilled literary craftsmanship of St. Luke. Dr. Armitage Robinson, for example, has said : [1]

" I see no reason for thinking that he used any pre-existing document at this point ; he was probably putting the story into writing for the first time, as the result of his own enquiries ; and his style is modelled on the old Hebrew stories, which he was familiar with through the Greek translation of the Old Testament."

In fact, as in his preface he imitated classical Greek, so in his account of the Nativity he imitated scriptural Hebrew. But it seems more likely that he was working upon and re-shaping with his accustomed skill some Aramaic document. When we find, for instance, such ritual details of the Purification as :

" When the days of their purification

[1] *Some Thoughts on the Incarnation*, p. 39.

according to the law of Moses were fulfilled, they brought him up to Jerusalem to present him to the Lord . . . and to offer a sacrifice according to that which is said in the law of the Lord, A pair of turtledoves or two young pigeons,"

most readers will feel inclined to agree with Dr. Sanday that this " is very unlike St. Luke, the disciple of St. Paul, the great opponent of everything legal, and very unlike the date A.D. 75–80, when the Christian Church had long given up Jewish usages." [1]

We must not pause longer over such details, interesting though they are. Let us sum up the impressions which, I suggest, we shall have derived from a careful reading of the opening chapters in the Third Gospel. We shall feel assured that St. Luke gives us the story of the Virgin Birth not as a

[1] *Critical Questions,* p. 135. I take the quotation from the late Dr. J. H. Bernard's *Studia Sacra,* which contains a paper on the Virgin Birth. Without undervaluing the work of Dr. Knowling or Bp. Gore's treatment of the subject in his *Dissertations,* and again more recently in the *S.P.C.K. Commentary,* I still do not hesitate to commend Dr. Bernard's paper in his *Studia Sacra* as by far the most lucid and convincing statement of the " conservative " view.

pious speculation, but as an historic fact, about the truth of which he has satisfied himself. We shall value the restraint and simple beauty of the writing. We shall recognize that much of it, if it be authentic, can have come from no one but the Mother of our Lord. We shall be convinced that St. Luke utilized, in part at least, some earlier Aramaic document. We shall note that the story of the Virgin Birth is told independently and confirmed by the Matthæan Gospel. And then, if we look beyond the New Testament period, we shall find that in the year A.D. 110, as a letter of Ignatius shows, the truth of the Virgin Birth was regarded as certain, as being on a parity with the truth of the Crucifixion.

Against such evidence is urged the absence of any explicit reference to the doctrine in the remaining two Gospels, the Acts, and the Epistles. I have said " explicit " reference, because various critics have held that in the Fourth Gospel and the Pauline letters are implicit allusions to the doctrine, and that even Mark is so phrased as not to be at variance with it. But there is no need to rely on such surmises. We can well understand why the Virgin Birth was kept secret during the early years ; even when it was published, some opponents of Christianity tried to give it a scandalous interpretation. We have seen how much there is to be said for the suggestion, supported by Dr. Streeter, that St. Luke himself was unacquainted with the story when he prepared the first draft of his Gospel, and that its present first two chapters were added by him subsequently. Thus the story of the Birth may well have been unknown to St. Peter and St. Paul. The author of the Fourth Gospel did know of it, in all probability, for he used St. Luke's Gospel. But his concern was to record those things which had come within the personal experience of St. John, those things which he had seen and known. Indeed, the argument of silence cuts both ways, for would he have kept silence had he heard the story and known it to be false ? We recall again the unhesitating statement of the doctrine among the Ephesians by Ignatius early in the second century. As Dr. Bernard remarks : [1]

" The Christianity of Ephesus owed much

---

[1] *Studia Sacra*, p. 193.

both to St. Paul and to St. John, and it is incredible that the Virgin Birth should have been a received dogma in that city so early as the year 110 if it had not been congruous with the well-remembered teaching of these great Apostles."

Such is the historic evidence for the Virgin Birth, obviously incomplete, yet good so far as it goes and unweakened by any substantial rebutting evidence. But the real battle-ground of the modern controversy lies elsewhere. Probably few people reject the doctrine because they are dissatisfied with the historical evidence, but a good many are dissatisfied with the evidence because antecedently they have found themselves unable to accept the doctrine. If we can credit nothing that is " supernatural," nothing that transcends normal human experience, plainly, we cannot believe in the Virgin Birth. But this attitude must invalidate belief in the Resurrection also, and in the sinlessness of our Lord. In fact, what we believe about Jesus is the fundamental issue. If He were merely human, not merely the first two chapters of Luke but the whole

scheme of the Christian faith becomes
incredible. If, in a unique sense, He
were divine, then the historic tradition that
His mode of entrance into this world was
unique is not one to which reason need
demur. The point has been admirably
stated by Dr. Headlam : [1]

" To sum up, then, the evidence for the
Virgin Birth is slight in quantity, but it
takes us back to an early stage in Christian
teaching. There is little or no evidence
against it. The evidence would not be
strong enough to justify our belief in it
if it were an isolated event apart from the
rest of the Gospel narrative. But if we
have convinced ourselves of the truth
of the Resurrection, of the Divine character
of our Lord's teaching, of the more than
human character of His life, then the further
account of His Birth harmonizes with that,
and the whole presents itself to us as a
record supernatural—unnatural, if you look
at the world from the naturalistic point
of view, but not unnatural if you look at
the world from the point of view of the
doctrine of the Incarnation, from the

[1] *Jesus Christ in History and Faith*, p. 179.

point of view of the whole Christian scheme.

There is no need to apologize, I hope, for having dealt with this subject at some little length, for it arises directly out of the first two chapters in Luke, and the controversy over it has disquieted many people anxious to understand the Gospels rightly. A full consideration of it would need, of course, far more than these few pages, but I have tried to set forth the chief points that must be taken into account. Just one more may be added as we pass from the subject. It is that the burden of proof must lie on those who urge us to abandon, not on those who retain, a belief in the Virgin Birth of Christ. If a friend of mine finds himself unable to accept the supernatural element in the Gospels, clearly he is compelled to reject the doctrine of the Virgin Birth, together with much else. That is, so to speak, his affair, and it is not for me to judge him. But that personal disability of his has no weight as an argument with other people. " The Virgin Birth," I am entitled to say to him, " is recorded independently as a fact by two of the Gospels. From at least the beginning of the second century, it has been believed by every branch of the Christian Church. It seems consonant with all that the Bible teaches of our Lord's nature, of His Incarnation and Resurrection. You cannot expect me to discard what has been an integral part of the Christian creed for eighteen centuries unless you can adduce some overwhelming evidence to justify such a step." That request cannot be met. There is no such evidence at all.

II

" The Gospel of the Infancy " in Luke is followed by another short section, consisting of chapters iii–iv. 13. Its theme is the preparation for our Lord's ministry ; the work of John, the Baptism, and the Temptation. Mark has only the briefest mention of these events ; Luke's source for this information about them seems to resemble that used in Matthew, yet it varies in some details. The temptations are given in a different order, and only in Luke do we find the Baptist's counsel to the multitude, the publicans, and the soldiers. Then in chapter iii. there is a genealogy of our Lord, widely different from that given in Matthew. Apart from lesser points, Matthew, the Gospel of the Messiah, traces our Lord's descent from Abraham ; Luke, the Gospel of the world-Saviour, traces it from Adam. We may be surprised to find the genealogy in the third chapter of Luke ; the more natural place for it would seem to be at the beginning of the Gospel, as we find it in Matthew. But its position rather strengthens the view that our chapter iii. in Luke was originally chapter i, and that the present chapters i. and ii. were a later addition.

Then follows, as in the two other synoptic Gospels, an account of the ministry in Galilee, iv. 14–ix. 50. All three virtually imply an earlier ministry in Judæa, but only the Fourth Gospel gives any account of it.

The Galilean ministry, as we saw in an earlier chapter, forms one of St. Mark's two main themes, filling almost nine chapters in his Gospel. St. Luke abridges considerably the sources used in Mark and Matthew, and rewrites their material in a more literary form. Yet often two of them, and occasionally all three, have a passage in virtually the same words.   As an example, the reader may look at the accounts of the healing of a paralytic in Capernaum : Mark ii. 1–12 ; Matthew ix. 1–8 ; and Luke v. 17–26.   In each Gospel is " But that ye may know that the Son of man hath power on earth to forgive sins (he saith to the sick of the palsy), I say unto thee, Arise," etc.   Thus, in each of the three Gospels, precisely the same parenthetic explanation is inserted in the middle of the saying of Jesus.   This seems convincing proof either that Matthew and Luke are copied from Mark, or that all three are copied from some one earlier document.

Certainly the common assumption that St. Luke as he wrote had before him the Mark Gospel in its present form does not become easier to credit as we look closely at the two books.   If he had the Second Gospel to consult, why does he omit so many details of a kind that would interest his readers ?   The story of the Syro-Phœnician woman is one that would appeal specially to the Gentiles for whom St. Luke was writing, but, though it is reproduced in Matthew, it is absent from Luke, together

with everything else between Mark vi. 45
and viii. 26. The attempts to explain this
great omission are unsatisfying. When St.
Luke begins again to narrate incidents
found in Mark also, it is at a point when
St. Peter figures prominently in the narrative. This supports another possibility.
Was his " source " not our Gospel of Mark,
but earlier " Memoirs of Peter " which
Mark had written before incorporating them
in a Gospel ? That is no more than a
conjecture ; yet the supposed direct use
of the Mark Gospel by St. Luke is also
only an hypothesis. I doubt if we can go
with confidence beyond the cautious statement of Dr. Plummer [1] that Luke has
" two main sources, (1) the narrative of
events, which he shares with Matthew and
Mark, and (2) the collection of discourses,
which he shares with Matthew."

I hope the reader will not think such
points dry and technical, of a kind to
interest expert students only. If we want
really to understand the Gospels, we shall
find it a great help not merely to read with
care each of them in turn, but to compare

[1] *International Critical Commentaries : St. Luke,*
p. xxiv.

each with the others. At a first glance, there might seem little to delay us in the section of Luke we are now considering, because by far the greater part of what it tells us about the Galilean ministry has been told already in Mark or Matthew or both. Yet, in a way, it is just such a section as this which reveals most of St. Luke's individuality. If we take the trouble to scrutinize his version with care, to notice the changes he makes from other versions, what details he omits and what he adds from his private information, what are the events and sayings he seems to regard as the most important, we come to appreciate far better than before his point of view and his special gifts as a writer.

In this section, too, we shall find (chapter vi. 17–end) the sermon " on a level place," which is at once so like and so unlike the Matthæan " sermon on the mount." Is it another version of the same discourse, or is it a quite different one ? That is hard to decide. On the one hand, we may be sure that our Lord often repeated the same teaching to different audiences. On the other hand, the Matthæan " sermon " does seem to be lengthened by many sayings spoken at various times, which the editor of Matthew, following his frequent plan, has " grouped." We shall notice that a large proportion of the sayings given consecutively in chapters v, vi, and vii of Matthew are scattered about at intervals over six chapters of Luke.

It is very interesting to compare the two versions of the Lord's Prayer given us by Matthew and Luke. Either St. Luke or the source he copied has abridged the form given in Matthew, and also altered some of the words. There are 57 Greek words in the Lord's Prayer as Matthew gives it ; of these 57 Luke uses 25, omits 22, and replaces the remaining 10 by other words. Are the two versions copied from different documents ? We might assume this but for one fact. In both the Luke and Matthew versions of the Lord's Prayer there is a word—the word translated " daily " in our English form—which occurs nowhere else. It is not found in the New Testament, or in ancient Greek literature, or in the papyri. It seems to have been coined for this single use, in order to represent some Aramaic term. As it appears in this one place only, the only clue we have to its meaning is its derivation, and this is uncertain. It is an adjective attached to " bread," and its most probable significance seems to be bread " for the time about to come " —i.e. " to-morrow." If so, the clause is not only, or indeed chiefly, a petition for our bodily needs, but for freedom from mental worry, from being " anxious for the morrow." That we may be spared that anxiety, we ask, not riches, but that we may have in store enough bread for to-morrow's need. Literally translated, the complete Prayer may be rendered :

Our Father in heaven !
As in heaven, so on earth
  Thy Name be reverenced,
  Thy Kingdom come,
  Thy Will be done.

Our bread for to-morrow give us to-day,
And forgive us our debts, for we forgive our debtors,
And bring us not into temptation, but deliver us from
 the evil one.

There is good reason for believing that the longer version of the Prayer, preserved by Matthew, is correct, but that the account in Luke of the occasion when it was given— in answer to a disciple's request—is accurate.

Of course it is possible, and indeed probable, that this was only one of many times that our Lord repeated the Prayer in the course of His travels and teaching.

III

Following the story of the work in Galilee comes a section of the Gospel we should read with special care, both because of its extreme beauty and because nearly all its contents are found in Luke alone. It extends from chapter ix. 51 to chapter xix. 28. It enables us to realize that the Master's final journey from Galilee to Jerusalem must have extended over a month or two—a fact not disclosed by Mark or Matthew. Some critics have discerned in this section signs of a feminine point of view, of a sympathy with the Samaritans, and of an acquaintance with Herod's court. These features have led them to suggest that St. Luke was indebted for his information to one of the faithful women who accompanied our Lord. And of these the most probable seems Joanna, the wife of one of Herod's officials. Yet, interesting as it may be, a conjecture of that kind is

not very important. Whatever the source
of St. Luke's information, the use made of
it is altogether his own. No part of his
writings shows his skill more convincingly.
It is worth while to read through these
chapters as if we were doing so for the
first time. However well we know them,
I think we shall be impressed more than
ever by St. Luke's quick sympathy, his
deft portraiture, his unerring eye for the
essential points of a story. Everyone
remembers, for instance, the domestic
vignette of Martha and Mary at Bethany.
The contrast between the sisters is quoted
continually, has become one of the most
familiar things in literature. But how
many people realize that the whole of the
story, from start to finish, fills no more than
five verses in our English Bible, that St.
Luke manages in his Greek to tell it all in
precisely ninety-seven words ? Into ten
verses, again, he is able to condense the
vivid story and character-sketch of Zac-
chæus. These are amazing feats, as every
man of letters will agree.

No less wonderful is the skill with which
the " atmosphere " is managed in that
section of the Gospel we are now consider-

ing. There is sunshine as well as shadow
in these chapters ; rejoicing crowds, and
happy, intimate friendships, and little
children brought for the Teacher's blessing.
Yet always in the background is the impend-
ing tragedy of the Passion, and we are made
to feel its awful and inexorable approach.
All this part of the Gospel may be termed
rightly a triumph of literary craftsmanship.
But we need accept no mechanical theory
of inspiration if we add that the man who
wrote these chapters was taught by the
Spirit of God !

The next section of the Gospel, describing
the last days of teaching in Jerusalem,
extends from chapter xix. 29 to the end of
chapter xxi. Then we have St. Luke's
account of the Passion in chapters xxii and
xxiii, and of the Resurrection and Ascension
in the final chapter, xxiv. These five and
a half chapters best produce their full
cumulative effect if we read them at one
time. Accordingly, the reader who follows
the scheme suggested here will study the
whole of Luke in four instalments : (1) the
Preface and Gospel of the Infancy (i. 11) ;
(2) the Galilean ministry (iii.–ix. 50) ;
(3) the ministry on the way to Jerusalem

(ix. 51–xix. 28) ; and (4) the last days,
Passion, and Resurrection (xix. 29–xxiv).

In the account of the last week in
Jerusalem we may notice that Luke, like
Matthew, shows no knowledge of Mark's
careful chronology, which tells us what
events happened on each day of Holy
Week.[1] Luke gives us no notes of time, but
changes the order of events very considerably. And it is clear that this Evangelist
had some independent sources of information for his story of the Passion. Were
it not for St. Luke, for instance, we should
be without the story of the penitent thief.
The other writers tell us only that the men
who were crucified with our Lord reproached
Him. But St. Luke relates how the one
rebuked the other, and prayed " Jesus,
remember me when thou comest in thy
kingdom." As St. Augustine observed,
some saw Jesus raise the dead, yet did not
believe ; the robber sees Him dying, yet
believes. And the reply, emphasized by its
" Verily I say unto thee," seems to many

[1] Professor Torm's comment is : " This circumstance
is by itself sufficient to raise serious doubt whether
Matthew and Luke have had our present Mark before
them."—*Church Quarterly Review,* July 1927.

of us one of the most precious sentences in the New Testament. " To-day shalt thou be with me in Paradise " is an explicit pledge that consciousness and personality persist through death. Not " thy spirit " merely, but " thou," the man himself, " shalt be with me." Few of us would willingly be bereft of that saying, and it is due to St. Luke alone that its comfort is ours.

IV

He has independent sources of information, again, for his narrative of the Resurrection appearances. Indeed, the apparent divergences of the Gospels at this point are striking. They have been, and are still, the theme of intricate discussion. Attempts to harmonize the different versions are often ingenious and sometimes plausible, but this is the most that can be said for them. The points they try to establish do not really admit either of proof or disproof, simply because the records are fragmentary, and we have not sufficient knowledge of the facts to justify a decided conclusion. On the other hand, it is fair to remark that discrepancies in detail do not invalidate the testimony of all the accounts to the one fact of overwhelming importance—that of the Resurrection itself. We can feel that the differences in the Gospels arise mainly from their incompleteness, while no discrepancies would have been allowed to appear if the story had been fabricated. Those are points we are fairly entitled to make. But we must not pretend that there are not two distinct traditions in the Gospels about the Resurrection appearances of our Lord.

It is the " Jerusalem tradition " that we find in Luke. If this Gospel (with Acts) were our only source of information, we should suppose that the risen Master showed Himself in or near Jerusalem and nowhere else. Also we should gather that His disciples were told not to leave Jerusalem, and remained there accordingly between Easter and Pentecost. When, however, we turn back to Mark and Matthew, we get a quite different impression. We learn that before His Passion our Lord said : " After I am raised up, I will go before you into Galilee " (Mk. xiv. 28 ; Matt. xxvi. 32), a saying omitted in Luke. Then, in the dawn of Easter Day, the message of the angel to the women is: "Tell his disciples and Peter, He goeth before you into Galilee : there shall ye see him, as he said unto you" (Mk. xvi. 7 ; Matt. xxviii. 7). Half-way through the next sentence the original Gospel of Mark is broken off, but in Matthew (xxviii. 16) we are told that "the eleven disciples went into Galilee, unto the mountain where Jesus had appointed them. And when they saw him, they worshipped him : but some doubted. And Jesus came to them and spake unto them. . . ." Here, then, in Mark and Matthew, we have the "Galilean tradition," in seeming variance with the "Jerusalem tradition" of Luke. But Luke is supported by John, which describes appearances in Jerusalem to the disciples on Easter Day and a week later. Yet in the appendix added subsequently to this Gospel (chapter xxi), we do find an account of an appearance in Galilee.

Such then, briefly stated, is the problem. St. Luke seems to know nothing of Resurrection appearances to the disciples in Galilee; the editor of Matthew seems to know nothing of appearances anywhere else. The existence of the "Jerusalem tradition" and of the "Galilean tradition" is indu-

bitable. When this is fully admitted, however, we have the right to add that the
existence of the two traditions does not
necessarily prove that one or the other must
be false. Rather we may think that both
are true. The Galilean appearances are
not disproved if no account of them happen
to be among St. Luke's materials. Again,
no one Evangelist could record all he had
heard, as the writer of the Fourth Gospel
pathetically insists. He had to make a
choice, and to omit much. In St. Luke's
final chapter, verses 44–50, evidently, are
much condensed. It looks as though the
writer found that the Emmaus story had
taken more space than he anticipated, so that
at its finish he was almost at the end of his
roll of papyrus. To those of the Gospels
we should add also the list of Resurrection
appearances given by St. Paul in I Cor. xv.
Its early date gives it great evidential value.
The Apostle cites it as one of the traditions
he " received," presumably about the time
of his conversion. That takes us back to a
time within six years of the Resurrection
itself. St. Paul mentions the appearance to
Peter, mentioned by St. Luke also ; a
" Jerusalem " appearance, and the appear-

ance to "above five hundred brethren at once," which must have been a "Galilean" appearance—for there were not that number of Christian brethren in Jerusalem before Pentecost.

Farther than this we need not try to go. Attempts to explain every detail, or to construct a kind of chronological table for the forty days between the Resurrection and Ascension are futile. We have not enough knowledge of the facts to justify such pious imaginative efforts. What we can say is that the stories of the Jerusalem appearances, and of the Emmaus scene in particular, ring true. It is reasonable also to think that the Apostles, taught by the Risen Master what their new life-work was to be, would need to return to Galilee for a short time in order to wind up their affairs, and that other manifestations of the Lord were given them there before they came back to Jerusalem. That the two traditions create a *prima facie* difficulty should be frankly admitted. Yet when it is examined without prejudice, the difficulty is not of a kind which demands the rejection of either tradition, or of any incident related in the Gospels. It is due merely to the incomplete-

ness of our information. If we want sufficient historical evidence in the Gospels to
support our religious belief in the Resurrection, we shall find it. If we require a
detailed and orderly account of everything
that happened in the last forty days of our
Lord's earthly life, we shall not find it, for
it is not there.

Certainly none of us could wish that St.
Luke, in order to say something about
Galilean appearances, should have abridged
that most beautiful narrative of the Emmaus
journey which is the last and possibly the
greatest treasure of his Gospel. From what
source did he get it ? As we read it carefully, as we notice its vivid and life-like
details, we cannot help feeling, I think, that
it is the record of a personal experience.
And as St. Luke is careful to name one of the
two pilgrims, while the other is unidentified,
the belief that the Evangelist got this
account from Cleopas himself seems one we
may accept. That matters little. What
does matter is the beauty of the tale, its
quiet power, the conviction it brings that it
goes far beyond the range of human invention. The summarized account of the final
charge and the Ascension follows ; of these

12

St. Luke was to say more in his later volume. But the story of the travellers on the road to Emmaus may well serve us as the epilogue to his Gospel. As we close it, I think we shall echo the pilgrims' words : " Did not our heart burn within us, while he talked with us in the way ? " Nor, as life goes on, are we likely to forget our gratitude to St. Luke for writing down :

" ' Abide with us : for it is toward evening, and the day is far spent.' "

" And he went in to abide with them."

I

As he passes from the first three Gospels
to the Fourth, every reader must be conscious of an essential difference. To some
extent, as we have seen, each of the synoptic
Gospels is individual in its purpose, contents,
and style.   But the point of view and atmosphere of this Fourth Gospel seem strikingly
unlike those which are common to the
others.   The contrast is evident even at a
casual glance through the book. Closer
study will show the reader that there are also
remarkable points of likeness, and he may
even come to share Dr. Scott Holland's
belief that " the Fourth Gospel, far from
being in collision with the other three, is
absolutely essential for their interpretation."[1]
Yet the great and obvious difference remains,
and has caused the Fourth Gospel in modern
times to be the most discussed book in the
Bible.

[1] *Creeds and Critics*, p. 86.

The discussion, too, is one of a kind which the general reader cannot afford to disregard. Details indeed there are which, though they have caused and continue to cause voluminous controversy, need not affect the profit and enjoyment with which most of us read the Fourth Gospel. Whether A.D. 90 or 105 is its more probable " date " ; whether it is essentially Hellenistic or Semitic in character ; whether or no the philosophy of its prologue has any affinity with that of Philo —these, and a number of other such questions, the general reader may leave to technical experts. The question of " authorship " is more important, especially if that word be given its right meaning. Yet it is still secondary. Were we driven to believe that we owe the book not to the son of Zebedee, but to another " John," or to an unknown disciple who somehow was present at the Last Supper, we might regret the overthrow of the older view, yet the historic and spiritual values of the book would remain unimpaired. Again, the great difficulties—personally, I do not think " overwhelming " too strong a term—against taking the Fourth Gospel and the Book of Revelation as the work of the same writer need not in any way perturb us. It is an interesting problem to investigate for people with sufficient leisure and technical equipment. But the decision, whichever way it be, is not of fundamental importance.

On the other hand, the main point raised by the modern controversy over the Fourth Gospel is of an importance quite fundamental. It is not of a kind that the general reader can view with unconcern or leave scholars to fight out among themselves. It must affect his whole estimate of the Fourth Gospel. Indeed, the question propounded is whether or no he can justly regard this work as a " Gospel " at all, for that term is one which seems incongruous to describe a work of pious imagination. A considerable number of writers would endorse Canon Streeter's statement [1] that the Fourth Gospel " belongs neither to history nor to biography, but to the library of devotion." Another believes that at the end of the first century the need was felt of a reinterpretation of the life of Christ in the light of Christian experience. Others suggest that it may most fitly be termed an allegory. In a paper contributed to *Cambridge Biblical*

[1] *The Four Gospels*, p. 365.

Essays, Dr. Inge says that " the whole book is a free composition by the writer himself," and that " the Discourses "—i.e. the teaching attributed to our Lord—" bear primarily on the conditions of Christian life in A.D. 100." It would be easy to add many other judgments of the same kind ; it would be no less easy to match them by the opinions of other critics, no less eminent, who take a precisely opposite view.

Enough has been said, however, to indicate the nature and the seriousness of the problem involved. This Fourth Gospel comes to us in the guise of history. It was accepted as historically true from the second century onwards. It affirms that Jesus Christ in the course of His life on earth did certain things and spoke certain words. Either He did and said those things, in which case the Fourth Gospel is the record of fact, or He did not, in which case it is a work of fiction. The latter alternative does not imply, of course, that its author wrote with any idea of deception. But the difference in the value of his book is immeasurable. Instead of preserving for us the words of Jesus Christ, it contains merely (in Dr. Inge's candid phrase) " free composition by the writer himself "—the kind of things he imagined our Lord might have said. He is not merely interpreting or expanding, but inventing. And, as Dr. Bernard remarks,[1] " It is one thing to spiritualize history ; it is quite another to put forth as history a narrative which is not based on fact."

When, therefore, we try to picture to ourselves the historic Christ and to study His teaching as a whole, may we use the material provided by the Fourth Gospel, or must we limit ourselves to the synoptic writings ? Is this book what, until modern times, the Christian Church always supposed it to be, or is it merely human, a beautiful meditation or allegory ? If so, we may value it as we value the *Imitation of Christ* or *The Pilgrim's Progress*, yet that is to place it on a level very different from a book recording, not what some devout soul invented, but what Jesus Christ actually said and did. Such is the enormously important question which confronts us. We are bound to face it. We must try to arrive at an answer. The general reader need not imagine that he is incompetent to

[1] *Commentary on St. John*, vol. i, p. lxxxvi.

do so because his scholastic equipment is small. A knowledge of human nature and psychology, an alert feeling for literature, and, above all, a devout mind are qualities quite as likely to help us as merely academic learning. The way to form a real opinion about the character of the book is to read it again and again.

And this we must try to do without pre-possessions. It is futile to pretend that the traditional view is free from difficulties, or that it must necessarily be right just because it is the traditional view. On the other hand, we ought not to be misled by the unjustifiable attitude of some modernists, who imply that none but the opinions they themselves hold are now possible for any person of intelligence. Some of them are apt to show a temper of unhappy intellectual arrogance, and to ignore, instead of trying to answer, evidence against their theories adduced by scholars of a competence at least equal to their own. This pose of having said the final word on the Johannine problem is not taken by all the radical critics. Yet it is too common, and has rather misled the general public. We must remember also that the historic worth of this Gospel is often disparaged because it cannot be reconciled with a certain type of modernist Christology. As Dr. Sanday observed long ago, " If a writer starts with a semi-Arian conception of Christianity, he is bound at all costs to rule out the Fourth Gospel, not only as a dogmatic authority, but as a record of historical fact."

II

We should try, then, to examine the Fourth Gospel without prepossessions. Two questions have to be considered ; those of its authorship and its authenticity. The latter, obviously, is by far the more important.

When we speak of " authorship," we should be careful to use that word in its right sense. To say that this book seems to be the Gospel of St. John the son of Zebedee is not necessarily to say that all the writing and arrangement of the book, as we now have it, were done by him. A modern analogy may help to explain the point. Two of the most valuable commentaries on my bookshelves, published at an interval of twenty years, are those on this Gospel by Archbishop Bernard (1928) and by

Bishop Brooke Foss Westcott (1908). Dr.
Bernard passed away in 1927, and therefore
his book, as the title-page states, was
" edited by " Dr. McNeile ; yet it is Dr.
Bernard's commentary. The other instance
is still more to the point. From his early
years Bishop Westcott planned a full
commentary on the Greek text of the
Fourth Gospel. He was already at work
upon it in 1859. But he was hindered from
the completion of his task by requests for
other books, among them a short commentary on the English version of John.
Afterwards he returned to the larger enter-
prise. He accomplished much of it between
1883 and 1887. In 1890 he became Bishop
of Durham ; after that, he could only give
fragments of time to his great commentary,
and it was incomplete when he died in
1901. Afterwards one of his sons set to
work upon the material bequeathed to
him. Of the twenty-one chapters in the
Gospel, the Bishop had re-annotated ten
fully and three partially. For the rest, his
son could use (*a*) the 1882 commentary on
the English text, and (*b*) a large mass of
disconnected notes. Using all these, he was
able, seven years after his father's death,

to bring out the splendid commentary in two volumes. Now it was the son who, in a literal sense, was the writer of this book. He made it ; he pieced together the materials, both chapters ready for press and rough notes ; he filled the gaps. Without him the book would not have existed. Yet, most properly, we term Bishop Westcott the " author," and his name only appears on the cover, for the whole substance of the book is his. It appeared seven years after his death, let us observe, and some of the notes first printed in 1908 had been put on paper forty years earlier.

That was the way in which a commentary on the Fourth Gospel came into being, and possibly that is not unlike the way, allowing for vastly different conditions, in which the Fourth Gospel itself was shaped. Beyond question, it had an editor as well as an author. Editorial notes are inserted in it, of which the most important comes at the close (xxi. 24). We should notice its wording carefully. There had been three references in the Gospel to an unnamed disciple " whom Jesus loved." The editorial note has two purposes : first, to let us know that from the reminiscences and

written memoirs of this disciple the Gospel
has been compiled ; secondly, to give a
certificate, probably on behalf of the elders
of the Church at Ephesus, of his veracity :

" This is the disciple which beareth
witness of these things, and wrote these
things : and we know that his witness
is true."

Such is the account contained in the Gospel
itself of the way in which it was fashioned.
An anonymous editor put it together,
from what a beloved disciple of Christ had
said and written down. The disciple must
have been a very old man by this time ;
but another editorial note (xix. 35) implies
that he was still living. Yet those written
notes of his, utilized in making the Gospel,
might have been set down long years previously ; his records of what the Master
said might have been committed to writing
within a short time, even within a few hours,
of the discourse itself.

Who, then, was this " beloved disciple " ?
He must have been an Apostle. He reclined
next to our Lord at the Last Supper. He
was one of the seven to whom the Resurrec-

tion appearance by the sea of Galilee was given. He survived to old age, and this fact gave rise to a misunderstanding which chapter xxi. was written to correct. All these points are consistent with the early and continuous tradition that he was St. John the Apostle, and there was no rival tradition at all. It seems significant that he is not mentioned by name in this Gospel. That is most difficult to explain unless he appears instead as " the disciple whom Jesus loved "—for a total lack of reference to him would be incredible. But, it has been asked, does not this argue against St. John's authorship of the book ? Would he have used so exalted a term as this as his way of describing himself ? There is undoubtedly some substance in that difficulty for those who think that St. John was the actual writer of the Gospel in its final shape. But if (as those believe whose views I share) it was compiled from his writings and reminiscences and edited by another hand, I can well think that the Apostle charged the editor not to mention him by name. Yet the editor had to describe him somehow, and, having learnt that " he whom Jesus loved " had been the proud title accorded to John by his companions, would use that mode of identifying him in the Gospel.

What is beyond controversy is that by the end of the second century this book was definitely accepted as a Gospel, equal in authority with the other three. Those who attack its authenticity point out how vastly different it is from the others in tone, character, and contents. That is quite true, but as an argument its weight seems to be rather on the other side. Would a work so markedly different have been allowed to rank with the others as a Gospel unless it had the compelling authority of an Apostle behind it ?

III

Such are a few of the many points that arise when the authorship of the Fourth Gospel is discussed. There seems no adequate reason for doubting that it is compiled and edited from the reminiscences and writings of the " beloved disciple," and if we are to reject the unanimous tradition of the Church [1] that the beloved disciple was

[1] Attempts have been made in modern times to show that John the son of Zebedee did not survive to

John the son of Zebedee, we have to find
someone else to take his place, and someone
of such authority that his records were
given the supreme rank of a Gospel. Dr.
Bernard favours the theory that " the
writer who compiled the Gospel on the
Apostle's authority " was also called John,
so that " we may find here a plausible
explanation for some confusion of him in
later times with his greater namesake." [1]
Yet, as we have seen when we were considering the analogous instance of Matthew,
the fact that afterwards the Fourth Gospel
was headed " according to John " does not
necessarily imply a belief that he was its
actual writer. " Matthew " was justly so
called, though another than St. Matthew
wrote it, because it enshrines the records of

old age in Ephesus, but was martyred early in Palestine,
and therefore could not have been the author of the
Gospel. This view, however, is opposed to all early
tradition, and the chief argument adduced for it is
what an eighth-century compiler says that a fourth-
century historian says that a second-century bishop
affirmed. It is evidence of a kind that no one would take
seriously unless, on quite other grounds, he had decided
against the traditional authorship of the Gospel. Dr.
Bernard has disposed of it most effectively in his
commentary (i, xxxvii–xlv.).

[1] *Commentary*, i, lxx.

our Lord's Discourses which St. Matthew
made. And "according to St. John," in
the same way, need not mean that St.
John wrote it—though through long
centuries the title was interpreted in that
sense—but that it contains what St. John
wrote. I do not think we press the editorial
phrase " the disciple which *beareth witness*
of these things, and *wrote* these things "
too far if we take it to imply that the
beloved disciple supplemented the written
records he had made long before with
verbal reminiscences which he was still
uttering in his extreme old age. The distinction of tenses seems to support that
interpretation, which is true to life and
human nature.

To determine the precise shares of author
and editor in the completed work is impossible. But the problem of its style is
interesting. The style is consistent throughout this Gospel; it is identical with the
style of " the First Epistle of John "; it
is very unlike the style of " the Revelation."
Assuming the matter of the Gospel to come
from St. John, is its manner his own or
his editor's ? Dr. Bernard takes the latter
view. Therefore, as the Gospel and First

Epistle are identical in style, he has to attribute the Epistle, not to St. John, but to the editor of the Gospel, whose name is also supposed to have been John. Frankly, this strikes me as incredible. The Epistle begins :

" That which was from the beginning, that which we have heard, that which we have seen with our eyes, that which we beheld, and our hands handled, concerning the Word of life . . . that which we have seen and heard, declare we unto you . . ."

Does not such language imply that the writer had been an eye-witness of our Lord's ministry ? And the whole letter— with its tender concern for the " little children " of a new generation, full-grown men and women though they be, its slow, ruminative tone, its repetitions and reitera- tions—seems of the kind a very old man would write or dictate. That is to say, it is such a letter as we should expect St. John to write, and by no means such as we should expect a young follower of his to address to his own contemporaries. Then we must remember that the Gospel, accord-

13

ing to its own statement, contains what the beloved disciple " wrote," as well as the verbal " witness " he gave his editor. It seems more probable that his pupil would assimilate the style of his own editorial notes to that of his master than that he would rewrite the documents handed to him by that master in a style of his own.

Behind this question lies another, far more intriguing. Let us suppose, as I think we have substantial reason for doing, that the idiom of the Fourth Gospel is the idiom of St. John—mainly his own, partly that of a disciple copying him. How far did St. John, in turn, mould his own style on that of his Divine Master ? The language in which His teaching is reported so closely resembles that of St. John's interpretation and comments that often we are puzzled to know where the one ends and the other begins. Therefore even those who believe that the Discourses have an historic background incline to think that their form is St. John's, that he set forth the substance of the teaching in his own idiom. Yet may not the reverse process possibly be true ? Given the beloved disciple's special intimacy with his Master, given his spiritual sensitive-

ness and his deep devotion, is it not psychologically probable that (almost without
knowing it) he acquired the habit of copying
the Master in his way of speaking about
religious truths ? If so, it is not the Discourses which are assimilated to the style
of St. John, but the style of St. John which
is assimilated to the Discourses. Here, no
doubt, we are in the realm of mere conjecture. But, personally, when I read such
teaching as is given in John xiv, with its
slow, tranquil, and most beautiful cadences,
such, I cannot help feeling, must have been
the kind of way in which our Lord spoke.
And when elsewhere in the Gospel I find
that the author's narrative and comments,
if on a lower plane, yet are in a diction not
unlike that he attributes to our Lord, they
seem natural enough if they come from a
disciple who was the readiest of learners.
One of the arguments used against the
Johannine authorship of the Fourth Gospel
is the alleged difficulty of attributing such
a work to a Galilean fishing-boat proprietor.
At best, the argument is not worth much.
It is akin to the plea that a Stratford peasant
could not have written *Hamlet.* One might
reply that, after all, exceptional people

sometimes appear in the world, and these exceptional people have a way of doing exceptional things. But in the instance of the beloved disciple something further may be added. There need be no cause for surprise if a Gospel unique and distinct in its beauty were written by a disciple who, beyond any other, knew what was the power of God's Spirit ; who, beyond any other, derived all else he knew from his knowledge of the mind of Christ.

I

AMONG the world's greatest writings there are some, and Luke is of the number, which reveal much of their beauty and charm at the first attentive reading we give them. There are others, and the Gospel of John is pre-eminent among them, which yield their chief treasures only if we are willing to return to them again and again. It is true that no one with any literary perception can even dip into this Fourth Gospel without feeling something of its fascination. Yet at first he may be misled easily by its effortless style, its consistently serene atmosphere, its lucidity of phrase. Almost it may seem to him a simple book. Yet if he will read it through and through, steeping himself in its contents, pondering its statements and their half-hidden implications, and comparing what it has to tell him with what he learns from other parts of the New Testament, these chapters will

197

stir in him an increasing amazement. Apart even from any theological prepossessions, he will, as a man of letters, begin to revere the Fourth Gospel as one of the supreme triumphs of literature. He will perceive the magnitude of the task which its author undertook, and his triumphant success in doing it.

There is the divine and transcendent Christ portrayed for us in St. Paul's writings and the Epistle to the Hebrews. There is the Jesus of Nazareth at work among the people of Galilee brought vividly before us by the first three Gospels. They, it is true, proclaim Him to be divine also, as the Epistles do not fail to proclaim His perfect humanity. None the less, we needs must be aware of a difference of emphasis, and a resultant contrast between the portraits. That difficulty is ended, that contrast fades away, as we study the Fourth Gospel. Here is the Master living and working among his simple-hearted companions, Who entered into their daily needs, Who could talk with and befriend with equal readiness a woman of Samaria or a Nicodemus, ruler in Israel. Mostly we see Him in a different setting of place, and mostly hear Him speaking of different themes, yet throughout we feel that the portrait in all four Gospels is consistent ; the same Personality stands forth in all. But with this feeling co-exists another. As we come to know the Jesus Christ revealed to us in the Fourth Gospel, we realize that the loftiest language of adoration applied to Him in the Epistles is not misplaced. The Jesus Christ of St. Mark's Gospel is seen to be convincingly one with the Jesus Christ of Pauline theology. And the Evangelist who, in a book so apparently simple, achieved that unifying interpretation for us accomplished one of the greatest feats that literature can show.

Again, as the reader ponders the sayings attributed to our Lord in this Gospel, he becomes more and more aware of the profound thought underlying their pellucid form. The things said go deep ; the implications from them go deeper still. If these are the veritable words of the Son of God, they add immensely to our knowledge of His mind, and there is no part of our life which they must not influence. If they are merely the inventions of some anonymous writer at Ephesus, our approach to them must be very different and their value is immeasurably lower. And therefore the question of the authenticity of this Gospel is of the utmost importance to us all. That is why everyone, and not technical students only, must try to form some conclusion about it. We shall best qualify ourselves for this by reading through the book from end to end with an alert mind, and noticing the impressions it makes upon us.

As we set about this, it is useful to have before us a general plan of the book. The best short analysis of it I know was provided by the late Mr. J. E. Symes in his *Evolution of the New Testament*,[1] and this, with some slight modifications, I will reproduce here :

Chapter I, 1–18. Prologue.

I, 19–IV, 54. The Lord reveals Himself to individuals—to the Baptist, Nathanael, disciples at Cana, Nicodemus, the woman of Samaria, a nobleman.

V–VII. He reveals Himself as the giver of a new Law, as a Healer and

[1] Murray, 1921,

Feeder of the multitude. Opposition begins from kinsmen and Pharisees.

VIII, 12–X, 42. Opposition grows. Jesus reveals Himself as Light of the World, Good Shepherd, Son of God. The Jews, therefore, try to stone Him.

XI. Opposition still increases. Jesus reveals Himself as the Resurrection and the Life. Raising of Lazarus.

XII. Greeks desire to see Him. Jews plot His death. The end of His public revelation of Himself.

XIII–XVII. The private revelation of Himself to the disciples in deeds, words, and prayer.

XVIII–XX. The Trial, Death, and Resurrection.

XXI. Epilogue.

Other commentators supply longer and more detailed analyses of the Gospel. But this suffices to bring out its main theme, the progressive self-revelation of our Lord. We should notice how dominant in it are the two words Light and Life. While, too, we have deduced from the previous Gospels the special purpose which each was written to fulfil, the author of the Fourth Gospel himself states explicitly the aim of his book. It was written, he says (xx. 31), " that ye may believe that Jesus is the Christ, the Son of God ; and that believing ye may have life in his name." His choice from a wealth of material was guided by this purpose ; he has chosen for record those events and words and " signs " which most clearly attest our Lord's divinity.

II

A few notes on the contents may be added. The Prologue, some scholars have suggested, is really a hymn, written, like the canticles in Luke, in the form of Hebrew poetry. Dr. Bernard has developed that idea, and suggests that in the hymn certain prose notes and explanations have been interpolated by the editor. These notes occupy verses 6–9, 12, 13, 15–17 of chapter i. Then the hymn itself, arranged in the parallel form of Hebrew verse, will read in English :

> In the beginning was the Word,
> And the Word was with God,
> And the Word was God.

The same was in the beginning with God.

In Him was life,
And the life was the light of men.

And the light shineth in darkness ;
And the darkness apprehended it not.

He was in the world,
And the world was made by Him,
And the world knew Him not.

He came unto His own,
And His own received Him not.

And the Word became flesh,
And dwelt among us,

And we beheld His glory,
Glory as of the only-begotten from the Father,

Full of grace and truth.

No man hath seen God at any time ;
The only-begotten Son, which is in the bosom
   of the Father,
He hath declared Him.

At the beginning of the first Epistle
of John there are evident references to this
hymn. It need not have been written by
St. John ; more probably it is quoted by
him as a prologue to his Gospel, just as a
modern writer will often quote a poem,

or some stanza from it, on a flyleaf of his book or as a heading to a chapter. It seems significant that " Word " (*logos*) is nowhere used of Christ in the Gospel itself.

That begins, after the Prologue, as if the author's first idea had been to give a day-by-day account of our Lord's ministry, based on a diary kept at the time. We have an account of a day, then (verse 29) " on the morrow " ; verse 35 " again on the morrow " ; verse 43 " on the morrow " ; and ii. 1, " on the third day." At least that seems to prove (unless we are reading fiction) that these narratives are based on written memoranda made somewhere about the year 30, and are not reminiscences first committed to writing about the year 90— the approximate date of the Gospel. No one would profess to remember after an interval of sixty years not merely what events happened but which happened on which day.

The conversation with Nicodemus in the third chapter is an example of an account in which it is difficult to know precisely where the words attributed to Christ end and the author's exposition of them begins.

On the whole, verse 16 seems to be this point, as the paragraphing in our Revised Version indicates; yet we cannot be sure. But how vividly the earlier sentences make us realize the interview—the cloaked Nicodemus stealing into the room lit only by an oil-lamp; the hint of condescension in " We—we of the Sanhedrin—admit thy claim to be a religious teacher " changing into the sheer bewilderment of " How can these things be ? " and the night-wind sighing in the trees. Even finer, as litera-ture, is the interview with the Woman of Samaria in the next chapter. There is not a flaw in the psychology of her portrait. If it be imaginary, how consummate an artist was he who drew it ! We should remark also that this Evangelist, whose aim as he states it is to show that Jesus is the Christ, the Son of God, tells us in this chapter that He was " wearied with his journey "—is not afraid, as the editor of Matthew was afraid, of words revealing the complete humanity of our Lord.

We may feel a sense of loss in learning that vii. 53–viii. 11, the story of " the woman taken in adultery," forms no real part of this Gospel. It is absent from all the oldest MSS., it is queried in many later ones where it is admitted, and the vocabulary and style are markedly different from those of the genuine Gospel. They resemble far more closely those of the synoptic writers. Yet, though it has no right place in John, we need not regard the story as spurious. It has inherent signs of truth, reference is made to it in a number of early writings, and we may accept it as a genuine piece of some independent tradition. In its present position, however, it is misplaced.

It is impossible so much as to mention here all the passages in the later chapters of the Fourth Gospel which abound with beauty. In particular, no hasty sketch could do justice to the three chapters (xiv–xvi) of Discourses on the eve of the Passion, or to the marvellous prayer which follows (xvii). They are among the supreme treasures of Christendom. As we read them, we may notice the suggestion, endorsed and developed by Dr. Bernard, that the present arrangement of their text does not represent the original order, and that more probably they should stand thus: xiii. 1–30 ; xv ; xvi ; xiii. 31-38 ; xiv ; xvii. In the same way many scholars hold that, earlier in the book, chapters v. and vi. have been transposed. No MSS. support these conjectures, yet possibly the original editor of the Gospel may have failed to arrange in their right sequence the materials given him by St. John. If we try the experiment of reading the debated chapters as placed by Dr. Bernard, we shall agree, I think, that the change seems to give us a more orderly and logical scheme of narrative and thought. On the other hand, I doubt if logical orderliness of that kind seemed so important to St. John as it does to modern critics. He was not, like St. Luke, trying to write a manual of history. He was an extremely old man, putting together reminiscences of a period sixty years earlier ; using bits of a diary he had kept then, scattered notes of special Discourses he had heard, existing Gospels written by others, and memories which he gave his editor as they came back to him ; wandering a little at times from narrative to his own thoughts, adding afterwards at a later stage some saying or incident he had forgotten when describing the stage of the ministry when it occurred ; unable to supply an exact chronology, except when his tattered diaries came to his assistance, and utterly unconcerned about logical arrangement, so long as he could leave behind him a portrait of the Master he loved and adored— that, I think, is the impression which this Fourth Gospel gives us of its author.

It seems beyond question that, as first designed, the book was meant to end with chapter xx, the climax of which is that wonderful scene when the most resolute of sceptics has to cry " My Lord and my God," and the last verse of which is a summary of the whole book's purpose. Then, most fortunately for us, a misunderstanding of the Risen Lord's saying about the future of the beloved disciple caused chapter xxi, full of beauty and psychological truth, to be appended as an Epilogue.

III

We have read again, let us assume, the Fourth Gospel. While the cumulative impression of it all is still vivid, let us return to the question of the book's authenticity. To put the issue plainly, have we been reading fact or fiction ? Is it, in the main, a record of fact, or is it a work of imagination ? We cannot allow the stark reality and urgency of that question to be masked by well-sounding phrases like "an idealized portrait of Christ," or "a spiritualized interpretation of His teaching." They do not tell us what we want to know. Those conversations with Nicodemus and the Woman of Samaria which we have been considering ; did they happen, or did they not ? That scene when Thomas worshipped his Lord and his God ; is it merely a piece of picturesque imagination ? "I and the Father are one " ; " he that believeth in Me shall never die " ; are those the words of Jesus Christ or the invention of someone at Ephesus ? Not scholars only, but everyone must be enormously concerned to know the truth about that. On the one hand, the Christian Church from the second century accepted the Gospel as authentic. On the other hand, its authenticity is dismissed as incredible by a number of prominent scholars to-day, although many remain its convinced upholders.

Into the more technical points at issue between them it would be impossible to enter in a volume of this kind.[1] But the

[1] The literature on the subject is immense. But the reader who wishes to acquaint himself with first-

main points are not technical. They are, that is to say, of a nature upon which the general reader, especially if he has an alert literary sense, is as competent to form an opinion as the academic expert. Neither he nor anyone else can, from the nature of the case, arrive at a certain and irrefutable conclusion. Were that possible, the controversy would be at an end. What he can do, however, and what for every reason he must try to do, is to determine for himself whether the balance of probability is on the side of the traditional or the modernist view. (It is convenient to use those terms, but many scholars support the " modernist " view of

rate statements, in a moderate compass, of the Johannine problem in its more technical aspects, may be strongly counselled to read : (1) Part III (pp. 361–481) of Dr. Streeter's *The Four Gospels* (Macmillan), a most able presentment of the " modernist " view ; and (2) pp. 62–147 of *The Son of Zebedee* (S.P.C.K.), by the Rev. H. P. V. Nunn, upholding the " traditional " view. The Archbishop of York (Dr. Temple) contributes a preface in which he describes it as " an impressive study." Mr. Nunn sets himself to answer Dr. Streeter, and does so in a style always · trenchant, and at times, perhaps, rather truculent. Yet no one should accept Dr. Streeter's conclusions, or even his premises, until he has considered how they stand the test of Mr. Nunn's searching and scholarly examination.

the Fourth Gospel without holding the
doctrinal opinions with which " modernism "
is commonly identified.)

What, then, is the modernist case against
the traditional view of the Fourth Gospel ?
It is based mainly upon the very remarkable
differences between this and the three
synoptic Gospels. " They are so numerous
and great," argues the modernist, " that
John clearly belongs to a different class of
literature from Mark, Matthew, and Luke.
Those three have a historical basis and are
authentic. John, written long afterwards,
is not. In fact, the synoptic and Johannine
traditions are so incompatible that you cannot accept them both. The synoptics represent our Lord's ministry as extending over
one or, possibly, two years, and as being
carried out in Galilee. John makes it
extend over three years, and gives us Jerusalem and the neighbourhood as its scene.
Characters prominent in the Fourth Gospel
are unmentioned by the other three. It is
inconceivable that all the synoptists should
have said not a word about a miracle so
amazing as the raising of Lazarus had that
story an historic foundation. On the other
hand, John leaves unrecorded some of the

chief events in our Lord's earthly life, such as the Virgin Birth, the Temptation, and the Transfiguration. But the supreme contrast is in the conflicting accounts of our Lord Himself and His teaching. In the first three Gospels He teaches by means of parables, using them to convey lessons of practical conduct and to set forth His doctrine of the Kingdom of God. It is quite a different Teacher whom we find in the Fourth Gospel. Here there is not one parable, but mystical discourses on the Son's eternal relationship with the Father, and, instead of a Master who forbids His disciples to disclose His Messiahship, one who emphasizes and proclaims it continually. There is no equivalent here to the Sermon on the Mount. The addresses in the Upper Room are of a length which could not have been memorized. Indeed, only one style is used in the Fourth Gospel, whether the speaker be our Lord Himself or Nicodemus or Pilate ; obviously, this style must be the writer's own. And that style belongs to the close of the first century. The author does not really give Christ's teaching, but (to quote Canon Streeter) what He ' would have taught had He been dealing with the problems confronting the Church at the time the Gospel was written.' In short, the book is not history, but a devout fantasy, a religious prose-poem."

Such, in outline, is the modernist's case. How does the traditionalist reply ? He might begin by referring his opponent to the text of the Gospel. " You ask us to consider this a work of pious imagination. But at least it professes to be history ; twice there is a solemn asseveration of its veracity. If your view be accurate, you have to postulate that the real writer invented, first, the ' beloved disciple ' to figure as the author, and then inserted an editor, to append a fictitious note most solemnly declaring that the beloved disciple was the author, and that his witness was true. No doubt there are, as you say, conspicuous differences between that Gospel and the other three. Yet you exaggerate the difficulty they cause. On the point of chronology, most scholars now admit that when John differs from the synoptic Gospels—as it does concerning the day of the Crucifixion—John is probably right and the synoptics in error. As to place, if the three describe a ministry in Galilee and the Fourth a ministry in Jerusalem, it does not follow that either has gone astray. In fact, there is much in the synoptic Gospels which cannot be explained unless, in addition to the Galilean ministry they record, there was also a Jerusalem ministry about which their writers had no detailed information. ' How often would I have gathered thy children together '—it is in Matthew and Luke that we find this lament over Jerusalem. Could we need clearer evidence that our Lord had spoken His message often, though vainly, in that city ?

" As, therefore, the first three Gospels deal mainly with the Galilean, the Fourth with the Jerusalem ministry, is it surprising that many personages appearing in the one narrative should not be found in the other ? Again, let us try to picture in the light of common sense what choice of material a writer in St. John's position would be likely to make. He was putting together his Gospel for a Church which possessed three already. Would it be rational to fill it with accounts of scenes and reports of teaching which had been included in one or more of the earlier works ? Would he not rather, of set purpose, omit most of these, intrinsically important as they might be, in order to have space for words and deeds which none of his predecessors had described.

"But you point out, and with justice, that the teaching attributed to our Lord by the first three Gospels on the one hand and the Fourth on the other is not merely different teaching but a different kind of teaching. That is, I admit, a substantial difficulty. Yet it is fair to point out that there were not only different kinds of teaching, but different kinds of listeners. To most, the practical instructions and the attractive parables would appeal greatly, while the more mystical Discourses would seem well-nigh meaningless. But St. John was a man of profound spiritual intuition and discernment. He would note down and cherish the profounder truths uttered by the Master ; truths clad in a form which would convey nothing to St. Peter ; which would never find their way through that Apostle into the Gospel of Mark and the synoptic tradition. As for the assertion that St. John has but one idiom for all his speakers, that, often as it has been repeated by the modernists, is quite un-justified. It ignores an immensely striking fact, mentioned in the article on this

Gospel in *Hastings' Dictionary of the Bible*
(ii. 719). Its writer points out that the
author of the Fourth Gospel puts into the
lips of our Lord no fewer than 145 words
which he never uses in his own person.
Again, there are 500 words which are
freely used by him in his own portions of
the Gospel, or in the utterances of other
speakers in it, not one of which does he
ever attribute to our Lord. Is not that
immensely significant? Apart from all
other considerations, does it not seem
incredible that someone should have
fabricated the narrative, fabricated the
Discourses attributed to Christ, and have
managed to preserve consistently so subtle
a difference of idiom between them? Who
was this superb imaginative artist, this
consummate literary craftsman? How is it
that his name is unknown, that his very
existence was never suspected until it had
to be assumed, in modern times, simply
to justify your theories?

"No; the differences between the first
three Gospels and the Fourth, great as they
are, certainly are not greater than we
might expect when we bear in mind that
the Fourth Gospel was written by a man

of very different temperament, and much
more spiritual insight, that he wrote at
a later time and would be eager to relate
what had not been told by the other
Evangelists, and that he wrote with the
special purpose of emphasizing the truth
of our Lord's divinity."

IV

Such, then, though again in outline only,
is the kind of reply which the traditionalist
would make to the modernist. How are
we to decide between them ?

Well, let us consider again the kind of
impression the book made on us as we read
it. For my own part, speaking as one
whose business it has been through a great
many years to examine and appraise
literature, both historical and imaginative,
I feel that this Gospel rings true. Occasionally there are details in it which seem
open to question. But, speaking generally,
I find it impossible to think that anyone
devised out of his own imagination the
incidents which it records. Even the most
marvellous (such as the raising of Lazarus)
are accompanied by small incidental touches
which it would be natural for an eye-witness

to remember, but which it would tax the powers of the greatest writer of fiction to invent. Again, the more closely I examine the Discourses attributed to our Lord, especially those in chapters xiv–xvi, the more impossible I feel it to be that any human being fabricated such matchless sayings. That they should have been recorded with anything like verbal exactness is a point of obvious difficulty. Such an explanation, for instance, as Professor Swete gave seems to me far from adequate :

" It is not, I think, unreasonable to suppose that words spoken on the last night of the Lord's life . . . produced an impression that could not be effaced ; that at the end of a long life one who was present found almost the very words still ringing in his ears." [1]

The length of the Discourses, and the interval of sixty years which, according to this theory, intervened between the hearing and the writing down of the words have to be taken into account. A more plausible suggestion, I venture to think, it is one I made some years ago in an

[1] Preface to *The Last Discourse and Prayer.*

earlier book of mine. According to this Gospel, on the day of the Crucifixion the beloved disciple was entrusted with the care of the Lord's Mother, and led her from the Cross to his own home. Picture them together on that evening. How would he comfort her ? What would be a more natural, indeed a more inevitable, way of attempting that than to let her hear what her Son had said only twenty-four hours earlier in the Upper Room ? " Let not your heart be troubled, neither let it be afraid. . . . I go to prepare a place for you. . . . Peace I leave with you, my peace I give unto you. . . ." Were there ever words of comfort to match those spoken in the Upper Room ? And so the disciple would tell the Mother of them, and write them down for her while they were yet fresh in his memory. That record could be most carefully preserved, and then, sixty years later, the disciple would incorporate it in his Gospel.

Obviously, this is no more than a conjecture, but it still seems to me a not unreasonable way of accounting for what certainly needs explanation.

While, however, the traditional view of

the Fourth Gospel has its difficulties, they may seem slight indeed by contrast with those which the modernist view involves. We have to assume some unknown disciple at Ephesus with a literary genius equal to Shakespeare's. We have to believe that, being a devout disciple, he invented out of his own head story after story about the Son of God, attributing to Him deeds He had never done, picturing scenes in which He never figured, and putting into His mouth words of the most tremendous import which, in point of fact, He never spoke. Did the writer wish his work to be regarded simply as a pious meditation or allegory, and not as a record of fact? On the contrary, he appended to it— pretending, to make the deception more effective, that it came from another hand— a most solemn affirmation that the witness of the book was true. Then he allowed it to go forth to the Church as a Gospel. Is that psychologically credible? But the marvels do not end here. Unlike as it was to the existing three, the Church accepted this book as a Gospel, and as derived from St. John the Apostle. It is a vast mistake to suppose that the Church of the first centuries was uncritical. The right of various books—among them 2 Peter, Jude, and the Revelation—to be included in the New Testament was keenly debated. But, outside one small and obscure sect, which (like some modern critics) was led to reject the Fourth Gospel because of antecedent objections to its Christology, this work was universally recognized as a Gospel, and as the Gospel of St. John. Is that likely to have happened if the work were really nothing but a devotional meditation written by an unknown hand ?

With these questions before us, we go back once more to the book itself ; we turn its pages ; we ponder what we read in them ; beyond all, we watch Jesus Christ as we find Him shown to us, and listen to the serene and ineffable wisdom of His words. As we do that, I believe that an intuition, worth more perhaps than any mere logical process, will lead us to a definite view about the author of this book. We may or we may not be convinced that the " beloved disciple " is one with St. John the Apostle. That, relatively, is unimport-ant. But our spiritual faculties, and not our intellects alone, will convince us, even if we doubt the identity of the author, concerning the authenticity of what he wrote. As we close his book, we shall echo the words about him which someone set down long ago, and say, " We know that his witness is true."

V

Here, pausing on my last page, I look back on this study of the Gospels, to realize how much it has left unsaid, in how slight a fashion it deals with its majestic theme. Yet there is comfort in the hope that it may move some readers to return, with some trifle of added interest or knowledge, to the Gospels themselves. There is no treasure in the world like them. There is nothing else which so illuminates life and death, and what lies beyond death. Yet the real meaning of the Gospels will not be disclosed to us if our interest in them be intellectual only. To look through them to the living Christ they reveal, to try resolutely to attune our own lives with the ideals they present—that is the way, that, in a true sense, is the only way, to understand the Gospels.

THE END